In the Shadow of Conquest

Islam in Colonial Northeast Africa

EDITED BY

SAID S. SAMATAR

The Red Sea Press, Inc.

Publishers & Distributors of Third World Books

297.0961
SAM

The Red Sea Press, Inc.
15 Industry Court
Trenton, New Jersey 08638

Copyright © 1992 by The Red Sea Press, Inc.
First Printing 1992

Book design and typesetting by Malcolm Litchfield
This book is composed in ITC Berkeley Oldstyle

Cover Illustration by Carles J. Juzang

Library of Congress Catalog Card Number: 91–60525

ISBN: 0–932415–69–5 Cloth
       0–932415–70–9 Paper

Contents

In the Shadow of Conquest

The Islamic Vision

and Colonial

Northeast Africa

SAID S. SAMATAR

D ESPITE ITS AMBITIOUS TITLE, this introduction aims at a modest
undertaking: It seeks to provide a general perspective to tie together the
various articles in this volume. Even so, the task is not easy. While sharing
a common faith—and by implication the world view of this faith—the
societies under consideration are so distant and diverse as to inhibit any
generalization about them. Perhaps this explains why, despite the metamor-
phosis of the field of African history over the last two decades from a cottage
industry to a mass-consumer enterprise, scholars have generally tended to
shy away from a transregional approach to common themes and problems in
African history. Instead, they have preferred to concentrate on local histories
and issues—an investigative strategy that may be described, for want of a
better term, as the "miniature approach" to African historiography. The
appeal of the miniature approach in part derives from the fact that it spares

scholars the challenges and pitfalls of having to integrate the histories of numerous regions with a view to presenting the large-scale historical picture necessary for an adequate understanding of the past. Instead, it enables them to focus, happily, on a "limited scope" and to draw an exhaustive, intimate portrait of it, thereby minimizing the risk of scholarly gaffes—and consequent embarrassment—while maximizing the chance to attain a "specialist status," a highly esteemed position among academics.

One of the melancholy consequences of the miniature approach is that while the monographic study of the African past has been witnessing boom times in recent years, only modest progress has been made on a supra-regional level—a matter that we are painfully reminded of whenever we attempt to select a textbook for an African history course. (It should be pointed out in passing that the scholastic preoccupation with monographic history, at the expense of an interregional one, is apparently a common pitfall in modern scholarship, if we are to judge by Gore Vidal's sneering remark dismissing contemporary historians as a little army of "scholar-squirrels.")[1]

This is not the place to complain about the imbalance between the local and the translocal in our study of African societies. Such a sentiment however does motivate two questions designed to facilitate the reader's appreciation of the order and character of the essays presented here: (1) What did the societies treated here have in common during the period under consideration? (2) To what extent did this commonality shape or condition the character of their response when they faced a transregional crisis—the Euro-Christian conquest?

A self-evident answer is that the vast majority of these societies were Muslim. To say this is to imply a great deal—among other things, that they shared the Islamic world view. This view includes the assumption that Muslim societies belong to a universal, divinely instituted community (the so-called *ummah*). Muslims therefore do not regard it as an exalted or exaggerated claim to assert that they have been assured in the Qur'an: "You have become the best community ever raised for mankind."[2] Best, be it remembered, not by ethnic distinction or racial superiority but by faith in God and by good works to the cosmic task of God's on-going plan to redeem humanity.

Among the various implications of this Qur'anic prophecy, which serious Muslims must (and do) take seriously, is the universal Muslim assumption of a "historic covenant" between God and the *ummah*. Briefly, the covenant involves a two-part contractual relationship of interdependent obligations between the divine and human.[3] God's part is to look out for the welfare of the *ummah*, nurturing it into physical and spiritual health and protecting it from harmful injury. God in this respect is seen to be bound by His sovereign integrity to remain the perpetual guardian of His people. Man's part of the bargain (as realized through the *ummah*), on the other hand, is to submit totally to God (hence Islam) as the sovereign Lord of the universe, to observe the divine percepts and, above all, never to wander off from the "Straight Path of Truth."

If Muslims are assured by their religion to count on God's protection so long as they live in accordance with His sacred laws, it follows then that their religion also warns them of the loss of that protection should they fail to observe the divine laws. It is small wonder, therefore, that at numerous times in Muslim history whenever cataclysmic events threatened the life of the Muslim community, sober Muslims have tended to interpret these events in terms of a grave breach in the equilibrium of the covenant—in terms, that is, of man's failure to obey and God's subsequent punishment. The way to regain divine favor, some Muslims have often reasoned, is to rededicate society anew in accordance with God's sacred laws.

The closing decades of the nineteenth century engulfed the Muslims of northeast Africa in a series of traumatizing events attendant upon European (and in the case of the Horn of Africa, Ethiopian) occupation. Everywhere, from the Horn to the Nile valley to the Maghrib, Muslims were defeated and subjected to Euro-Christian rule; their lands were seized, their property plundered, their Islamic polity disrupted and their world view ridiculed as primitive and fatalistic.[4] Thus, humiliated and bruised, African Muslims at the turn of the century, like Muslims elsewhere, had good reason to wonder whether their objective reality justified their view of themselves as "the best community ever raised for mankind."

Given the intimate bond between their religion and their politics, the

Muslims' political reaction to European conquest must necessarily have been shaped by the imperatives of their religion. It is not irrelevant, therefore, to assess the "Islamic element" in the complex range of responses of Muslim northeast Africans to European aggression. J. S. Trimingham[5] and B. G. Martin[6], at any rate, do not think it irrelevant. Though different in style and temperament, their works nevertheless represent an instructive example of what could be achieved by way of a transregional approach. They both see the Islamic element as looming very large in the kinds of responses with which Muslim Africans faced European intrusion. They both underline the importance of Islamic reform and revivalism, which they claim fired many of the anticolonial movements of the time. Islamic revivalism, moreover, is seen to have served as the driving force behind many of the Sufi (mystical) movements that sprang up in the region towards the end of the nineteenth century. Some of these, like the Saalihiya of Sayyid Muhammad 'Abdille Hasan of Somalia, Amir 'Abdulgadir's Algerian movement of an earlier period, and (to take a distant example) al-Hajj 'Umar's Tijaniya in what is now Senegal were militant brotherhoods that took the sword to implement their vision of the ideal society. Others, like the Uwaysiya of Sheikh Uways al-Baraawe of Somalia and the Senusis of Libya were moderates who stopped short of advocating a direct *jihad* (holy war). They nevertheless displayed a millenarian fervor by which they sought to rededicate society and to point the way to a coming millennium.

Martin's and Trimingham's model of a revivalist, Sufi-led movement as constituting a common theme in the response of Muslims to European conquest has much to commend it, especially from the standpoint of explanatory ease and theoretical coherence. Indeed we feel a tempting urge to adopt their scheme as an all-purpose analytical tool in order to impose a degree of theoretical unity and consistency on this fragmentary exploration of certain areas of colonial northeast Africa. However, the data at our disposal resist such an approach, perhaps not regrettably. What the seven essays that follow do is to present seven case studies dealing with *aspects* of, rather than a common, Muslim response to the onset of European conquest. Furthermore, five of the seven provide fresh material (and this, we think, constitutes their principal contribution) on areas or individuals of considerable human and historical interest.

Of the two articles on the Sudan, one notably Dr. Lidwien Kaptiejns', examines the phenomenon of Muslim response at the state level, while the other, Professor Jay Spaulding's, looks at the same problem from the vantage point of the individual. They put forward, with insight and ability, interesting and contrasting perspectives. Dr. Kapteijns' study of Dar Sila, a "periphery" state that almost from its inception led a precarious existence between the larger sultanates of Dár Fur (in what was to become western Sudan) and Wadai (eastern Chad), goes far beyond a mere recounting of how a small Muslim state attempted to cope with the French threat. Her analysis undertakes a full-fledged reconstruction of the history of Dar Sila, covering such matters as the origins and growth of the state, its internal power structure, its foreign relations, and economic base. This usefully prepares the reader for the more rounded discussion of the events leading up to the French annexation.

By contrast Jay Spaulding's brief but perceptive study focuses on a "Letter" from one Sudanese "holy man" to another. The letter's contents (thanks to Dr. Spaulding's elucidation of their context) powerfully reveal the traumatic impact attendant upon the two religious dignitaries in their humiliating search for a way to come to terms with the rule of the British Raj. Even as they devise strategies to hold onto their household servants and domestic slaves (who had been suddenly and arbitrarily manumitted by the British), they betray a sense of helplessness and despair before the new order of things. Dr. Spaulding treats their collapsing world with competence and sympathy.

Abdusamad Ahmad's piece on the Muslims of Gondar (northwestern Ethiopia) rests not so much on any revelation of a Muslim response to Christian rule as on the improbable survival of a thriving Muslim community in the heartland of Christian Abyssinia. Muslim "survival institutions"— Qur'anic schools, catechistic liturgy, observance of religious festivals and near monopoly on trade—are discussed here in useful detail. Mr. Ahmad's history training, command of the prerequisite languages, access to relevant archives, and his indigenous (Muslim) roots in northern Ethiopia uniquely qualify him to recount the history of the Muslims of this region. One regrets that his study is confined to the circumscribed world of Gondari Muslims; he could, for example, fruitfully enlighten us on how the Muslim minority in Ethiopian highlands endured the cataclysms (recurrent famines, genocidal civil wars, and virulent dynastic struggles) of the second half of the nineteenth century. Of special significance here would be an examination, however brief, of the ways in which the Muslims of Wallo, Tigre, and Begemder provinces coped with Emperor Yohannes IV's sustained policy of forced conversion of Muslims to Christianity. Perhaps this is an unfair complaint. Still, Mr. Ahmad's study makes an important start towards filling a yawning gap in our understanding of Islam in the central lands of Christian Ethiopia.

Mohammed Hassen's essay deals with the Oromo Muslims of Wallo, a region in which Islam clearly has long roots, as Dr. Hassen's article amply demonstrates. His scholarship and indigenous roots as a native Oromo himself gives him a masterly command point from which to inform us on Islam, the Oromo, and Ethiopian Christian emperors' sustained attempts to forcibly convert the Oromo to Christianity. The result is indeed an informative piece of scholarship.

Of the three essays on Somalia, B. G. Martin's deals with the life and historical significance in Somalia of the great mystic and revered "miracle worker" Sheikh 'Abdirahman al-Zayli'i. To appreciate the timely contribution of this scholarly and meticulously researched essay, it is necessary to explain that the great majority of the Somalis (perhaps as many as 75 percent) belong to the Qaadiriya mystical order (the rest are members of the Ahmadiya, Saalihiya, and various marginal sects). In the nineteenth century Sheikh Sayli'i and Sheikh Uways between them dominated the world of Qaadiriya Islam in Somalia. As a result, and in keeping with the practice and precedence of Muslim spiritual leaders of mystical brotherhoods throughout the world, both gave rise to religious sects that, to this day, bear their names. In chronicling and interpreting this hitherto neglected portion of Somali Islam, B. G. Martin deploys all his usual tricks of the trade—his consummate command of Arabic to cull vital information from obscure and otherwise inaccessible fragmentary bits and pieces of material, his authoritative familiarity with theological and doctrinal controversies bedeviling the Muslim world, and his vast knowledge of African Islam generally—to offer a lucid reconstruction of the main outline of the life and times of this venerable mystic. His essay adds stellar quality to the book.

Mr. Abdul Samad Bemath's article on the other hand, covers familiar ground, notably Sayyid Muhammad 'Abdille Hasan's war of resistance against Ethiopian and British conquest of the Somali peninsula. Mr. Bemath's voice, both as a new student of the Somali Dervishes and as a young South African Muslim, resounds with a certain enthusiasm that commends itself for freshness and delicacy. His is a welcome addition to the collection.

My own contribution is a tentative sketch of the life of Sheikh Uways Muhammad of Baraawe, a less known but no less important southern Somali religious leader who, unlike the Sayyid, chose the path of mysticism and quiet piety as a way to come to terms with Euro-Christian conquest. Conventional wisdom in Somali historical circles has for long tended to dismiss Sheikh Uways's "withdrawal" strategy as no more than defeatist. My article aims to challenge this view by arguing, rather provocatively, that Sheikh Uways's revivalist movement had the greater positive impact on Somali society than the Sayyid's bellicose Saalihiya sect. This is a revisionist attempt designed to generate a fresh debate on the respective contributions of the Sayyid and the Sheikh to Somali national identity.

We hope, finally, that these essays, collectively, will add to our knowledge of the different ways in which African Muslims at the end of the nineteenth century reacted to the challenge of European colonial intervention. We also cherish the ardent wish that the book will contribute, in a small way, to our understanding of the evolution of African colonial society in general.

Notes

1. Gore Vidal. *The New York Review of Books.* Vol. 35, No. 7, April 28, 1988, pp. 55–57.
2. *The Qur'an,* Sura III: 110.

3. For the discussion of ideas of the "historic covenant," I have relied heavily on the Iranian scholar Seyyed Hossein Nasr's exposition of the subject in *Ideals and Realities of Islam*. Boston, Mass.: Beacon Press, 1975 Edn., pp. 15–65.

4. This theme receives short but helpful treatment in B.G. Martin, *Muslim Brotherhoods in Nineteenth Century Africa*. Cambridge: Cambridge University Press, 1976, pp. 2–3; 6–7.

5. J. S. Trimingham, *The Sufi Orders in Islam*. Oxford: Oxford University Press, 1971.

6. Martin, *Muslim Brotherhoods*.

CHAPTER ONE

Shaykh Zayla'i and the Nineteenth-Century Somali Qadiriya

B. G. MARTIN

O NE OF THE FEATURES OF THE nineteenth-century Somali landscape, in most parts of that country, and also in the Somali-speaking regions now under Ethiopian control, was wandering groups of adherents to Muslim brotherhoods who traversed the countryside seeking new followers for their organizations and, in non-Muslim regions, making converts to Islam. Invariably they had a leader, a *shaykh,* a charismatic figure who preached to the people and who listened to personal problems. In addition, many of these itinerant religious figures or *wadaads* had settlements of their own, where those who came to their little colonies (called a *jama'a* in Arabic) might eventually settle on community land, live a more religiously oriented existence than other Somalis, cultivate crops, and raise animals. Between the two main brotherhoods in nineteenth-century Somalia, the Qadiriya and the Salihiya, there were a large number of these *jama'as,* north and south, with a concentration of Saalihi brotherhood settlements roughly in the north and east, while the Qadiriya were more widely spread out. Three of the better-known Qadiri settlements were at Berdera (or Baardheere) on the lower Juba, another at Biolay, 150 miles northeast of Brava (Baraawe), and a third center at Qulunqul (or Kolonkol) in the Ogaadeen region near the south edge of the Harar plateau.

As yet, many of the local Somali religious leaders of this period are poorly known, if they are known at all. This is not true of Muhammad 'Abdallah Hasan of the Saalihiya, nor the Qadiri Shaykh Uways (or Awis) of Brava, leaders of the two major opposing brotherhoods. There had been others also, *wadaads* of the Dandarawiya, Rifa'iya, Rashidiya, and other minor orders. Nevertheless, these smaller competing organizations had far fewer adherents throughout the country than the Qadiris or the Saalihis. The Qadiriya was an old-established group that had been in Somalia since at least 1500, while the Saalihiya was an outgrowth of the Rashidiya *tariqa,* part of a cluster of new religious organizations inspired by the famous Shaykh Ahmad ibn Idris (born 1758), a Moroccan who had moved to Mecca and then to Sabya in Asir (formerly in Yaman but now in Sa'udi Arabia), where he died in 1837.

It would be no exaggeration to say that Idris's presence, as well as the lively theological and religious activity revolving around the great Yamani *qadi* (judge) and theologian Muhammad b. 'Ali al-Shawkani (1760–1834) not only gave a strong impetus to the Rashidiya brotherhood but helped accelerate the activities of other and older *tariqas* as well.[1] Many members of the Yamani *'ulama* (learned men) class—although Zaydis at this time—had ties to Zayla' and its hinterland, to the towns of Berbera and Hargeisa, and throughout the "Jabart" region.[2] It seems possible that Qadiri influence, no doubt intensified by its Yamani contacts, might be responsible for the still enigmatic episode of the alleged Qadiri community of Bardheere (ca. 1820) and the uncertain antecedents of its leader, Shaykh Ibrahim Jabaro or Jibirow. The Bardheere affair deserves further research to clarify its relations to other political and religious movements of the period.[3]

Yet the largest Qadiri concentration, where this *tariqa* was best rooted and had the most supporters, was in northwestern Somalia and adjoining parts of Ethiopia, centering around the towns of Harar, Jigjiga, and Hargaysa (or Hargeisa), likewise at Qulunqul in the Ogaadeen region (with the exception of Hargaysa, all of these places are now in Ethiopia). This northern Qadiri nucleus included several groups, each with its leader, but the Qulunqul (or Kolonkol) group was closely associated with Shaykh Zayla'i, since his tomb is situated there, and since he once had an agricultural settlement or *jama'a* there.

Shaykh 'Abd al-Rahman ibn Ahmad al-Zayla'i (b. ca. 1820, d. 1882) has been little known until recently—save for the date of his death and his burial, and an occasional remark by an author or two that he wrote poetry, worked miracles, and was considered a Qadiri saint of great importance. More information about him is now available but unfortunately only in a fragmented and incomplete fashion. This new information comes from an Arabic source, a compilation of Zayla'i's *manaqib* (singular *manqaba*). The usual meaning of this word is "divine graces" or "partial miracles," but sometimes the material in this account is anecdotal or biographical or simply folkloric.

The genesis of this book, called *Rahat al-Qalb al-Mutawali' fi manaqib al-Shaykh 'Abd al-Rahman al-Zayla'i (Relief for the Passionate Heart among the divine graces of . . . al-Zayla'i)*, is quite unexpected.[4] On Saturday night, 22 Rabi I 1371/17 January 1952, a Qadiri "brother" from Brava had a dream in which Shaykh Zayla'i appeared to him, suggesting that his *manaqib* be collected and be read every year at his tomb, from the first to the fifth of Rabi II, the anniversary of his death in 1299/1882. Ahmad ibn Hajj Habib al-Da'firadhi of Brava, who had this dream, turned the task over to several others, who eventually collected eighty-four *manaqib*, "drawn from the learned, and the mouths of men, and from the loving brothers of the *tariqa*." This plan was followed by the compilers, and Zayla'i's *manaqib* were eventually published in Cairo in printed form in 1954.[5]

Through a careful sifting of the materials in these *manaqib*, a rough biographical framework of Zayla'i's life can be constructed. The poetic can be separated from the real, the real from the supernatural or paranormal, and the folklore from the abundant literary material added by Zayla'i's admirers.

In addition to the eighty-four *manaqib*, there are a number of poems, mostly *qasidas*, by Zayla'i himself. Some poetical efforts by his followers and students are included with some useful commentary by the book's compiler, Shaykh 'Abd al-Rahman bin Shaykh 'Umar al-Qadiri.

A date (ca. 1820) for the saint's birth can be established from a claim (*manqaba* 72) that Zayla'i and Ibrahim al-Rashid, one of Ahmad ibn Idris's close associates, met in a garden for conversation, in the course of which Rashid told Zayla'i that he, Rashid, was the elder.[6] As Rashid's dates are 1228–91/1813–74, this information seems likely to be correct. Zayla'i was probably just over sixty when he died in 1299/1882. This information, according to the *Rahat al-Qalb*, is furnished by a member of the Qutbi clan, close associates of Zayla'i, a subject to be discussed further below.[7]

Zayla'i's origins also offer some surprises. Although his *nisba*[8] suggests that he came from the famous Somali town on the south side of the Gulf of Aden, the *Rahat al-Qalb* states that the saint's ancestors hailed from another Zayla', a village in Yaman adjoining Luhayya, a place "where many saints lived"; Shaykh Zayla'i's origin "was from them."[9] Although the compiler hints here at a mixed Somali and Arab ancestry, he states that Zayla'i was born in the Dasu clan among the Rahanwayn (or Rahanwiin), at a place called Gidle (or Kidle) in southern Somalia, situated about 100 miles northwest of Mogadishu.[10] It is expressly stated in *manqaba* 84 that Zayla'i was a person of humble origins. It is also stated that he was a person who did not fear encounters with other learned men or with sultans, and that he was accustomed to the society of poor people. As the compiler says, quoting a line from the North African mystic Abu Madyan Shu'ayb al-Andalusi,

> What is the deliciousness of life
> Unless it is in the company of the poor?
> [For] they are *sultans, sayyids,* and *amirs.. . .*[11]

Little is known of Zayla'i's family, and the compiler of the *Rahat al-Qalb* seems to be slightly confused about this point. *Manqaba* 17 mentions a wife called Radiya, and *manqaba* 53 mentions Zayla'i having a wife while he went off to Mogadishu to study, but nowhere is her name mentioned. Zayla'i did, however, have two daughters by her. This fact led on to a family crisis for Zayla'i, since the *manqaba* claims that the learned men of the Dasu clan "severed" Zayla'i's wife (Radiya?) from him, perhaps a divorce brought about by his long absence. One of his daughters (*manqaba* 54) died as a child, but the other survived. Whether or not this is the lady called "Shaykha Fatima bint Shaykh Zayla'i" (*manqabas* 36 and 38) is uncertain. *Manqaba* 75 mentions another woman, Fatima al-Ishaqiya, as being a wife of Zayla'i. Whether these two, Radiya and Fatima al-Ishaqiya, were co-wives or successive wives is unclear. In any case, the fact that Zayla'i evidently had no sons explains why, to use Trimingham's phrase, the Zayla'iya did not become a "family *tariqa*" but passed into the hands of the Qutbis. Yet Zayla'i was much annoyed by the compulsory divorce maneuvered by the Dasu *'ulama,* so he laid a curse (*da'wa*) on them; as a result, they all "died young."[12]

As a boy, Zayla'i had shown early signs of his mystical inclinations. At the Qur'an school (*manqaba* 22) he would play with other children, but sometimes went to a local cemetery, warning them to keep away from him:

> He forbade them and said, "Don't follow me." However, they refused. When they got to the tombs, a strong and very gusty wind sprang up, hiding him from them, and they ran away saying, "The wind has carried him off." Yet he came back after that without injury, because he was learning the sciences from the people buried there, and others. . . .[13]

Zayla'i's education is further outlined in the *Rahat al-Qalb*. He received elementary training in the Islamic sciences and in the *Qur'an* in his home district from the local *'ulama* and *shaykhs*. Very soon, he felt the need for a "perfect *shaykh*," a guide and *murshid* (spiritual guide) to lead and educate him. As mentioned, Zayla'i had difficulties with some of the local *'ulama* just after this time (*manqaba* 53).[14] These were probably the reasons that impelled him to set off for Mogadishu, "that mine of knowledge and blessing," to meet a man who would be his *shaykh* and mentor along the Sufi path. Yet he did

not do this without an *ishara* (sign). On arriving at Mogadishu he encoun-
tered among its numerous learned men Shaykh Abu Bakr ibn Mihdar and
Shaykh Sufi. For a time Zayla'i attended Sufi's classes and his *majlis*.[15] At this
time already, Zayla'i became ecstatic (*majdhub*) as he heard the name of the
Prophet mentioned, and *manqaba* 3 states that he had already seen the
Prophet Muhammad forty-four times, and then saw him again at the door of
Shaykh Sufi's house. Zayla'i lost the power to stand, and fell over in a faint.
At that, "Shaykh Ahmad ibn Shaykh Mahd took him by the hand and led
him to his house, treating him well."[16]

After a year or more in Mogadishu, Zayla'i met Shaykh Isma'il b. 'Umar
al-Maqdashi, a shaykh of "the exalted Qadiri brotherhood." Immediately on
seeing Shaykh Isma'il, Zayla'i followed and served him, washing his clothes
and carrying his slippers. After Zayla'i was accepted by the shaykh, the two
journeyed to Isma'il's home district, spending some time there with Isma'il's
own shaykh, Sayyid Hamza bin Mahumud al-'Awsi, taking an *ijaza* (permission to teach) from him. Whether or not this journey led them to the Awsa
region south and west of Zayla' (in Somaliland) is unclear from this account.[17]

Isma'il al-Maqdashi continued to teach Zayla'i about Sufi matters, and
when he had finished, he decided to test Zayla'i's character. He made Zayla'i
his camel boy, instructing him to guard his animals and so increase the
numbers of his herd, some of which he gave away as alms. One day, al-
Maqdashi told Zayla'i to make him a hut (*bayt*) of sticks and branches. He
asked Zayla'i to make a second hut, then a third one. Zayla'i's spiritual
powers soon began to manifest themselves; very shortly the branches of the
last hut began to arrange themselves without his touching them, over his
head. Noticing this, Isma'il al-Maqdashi told him that his period of testing
and serving him was over, and that Zayla'i needed to go to Mecca on the *hajj*
(pilgrimage). Al-Maqdashi told him to enter Mecca by a specific gate, and
that once there he would meet one of the descendants of the founder of the
Qadiriya, 'Abd al-Qadir al-Jilani (died 1166) and that this man, Sayyid Fadl,
would give him the Qadiri *silsila* (chain) of spiritual descent and an *ijaza*.
(Ultimately, Isma'il al-Maqdashi would designate Zayla'i as his successor in

the brotherhood.) Then, according to the *Rahat al-Qalb*, Zayla'i went to Mecca and stayed there "as long as God wished." Later, he returned home to Somalia via Harar, using the same route he had taken to reach Mecca initially. There are no further details of his education.[18]

At Harar, Zayla'i was questioned apparently by the local men of learning about his knowledge generally; they also asked him to write a commentary on the *Shatibiya*, a well-known treatise on the seven ways of reading the Qur'an, along with information about pronouncing certain words.[19] Zayla'i was able to do this in an appropriate way. He then composed a rhyming treatise on Arabic morphology (*'Ilm al-sarf*), as the local students were tired of reading their old text. Zayla'i's poem, *Hadiqat al-tasrif*, was seen to be very satisfactory and was eventually printed.[20] At this point, says the compiler of the *Rahat al-Qalb*, Zayla'i's prestige became "well diffused" and his reputation "spread as far as the horizons," and his rank was raised "in the towns and countryside." Zayla'i was now the center of one of the several Qadiri movements of northern Somalia (soon called the Zayla'iya after him), occasionally going to other places, but generally remaining in the neighborhood of Qulunqul or Kolonkol, and returning there after journeys or excursions elsewhere. The compiler of the *Rahat al-Qalb* claims that Zayla'i was "high above" his other contemporaries in learning and in spiritual guidance, and also in matters that are paranormal, or that "transcend the rational" (*khawariq al-adat*). Finally, 'Abd al-Rahman b. 'Umar tells his readers that Zayla'i's influence caused the Qadiri *tariqa* to spread "on Somali soil and elsewhere," and in certain of the ports (*banadir*).[21]

Zayla'i died aged about sixty-two, and was buried at Qulunqul. The date of his death is certain (5 Rabi II 1299/24 February 1882), for it is enshrined in a poem written by one of his followers.[22] (The author of the *Rahat al-Qalb* attributes remarkable powers to Zayla'i's tomb, although it is described repeatedly as being situated in a "dangerous place" [*manqaba* 63] and a remote one. Presumably this is so because Kolonkol was well within Ethiopia.) In any case, the tomb was soon renowned as "the refuge of the traveler, and the troubled and those in need." "Whoever visits it," asserts the compiler of the *Rahat al-Qalb*, "obtains what we have described [here], and many divine favors (*karamat*) have occurred which cannot be counted or enumerated."[23] For some of these, see page 26 below.

After al-Zayla'i had completed his education at Mogadishu and in Mecca, he doubtless returned for a time to his home town of Gidle (or Kidle). Then, as *manqaba* 51 states, he applied to his *murshid*, his *shaykh*, Isma'il al-Maqdishi, for permission to go to Muhammad Zubayr territory to spread the Qadiri *tariqa* and its *dhikrs*.[24] In the late 1850s or early 1860s, a very approximate date for Zayla'i's arrival in the Ogaadeen and his first stay at Kolonkol (whether he founded his *tariqa* settlement there, his *jama'a*, at this time is problematical) the Muhammad Zubayr pastoralists had not yet moved to their present location, further south along the lower Juba. They arrived in that region only after heavy Ethiopian raids and constant military pressures in the 1880s. However, in the Ogaadeen "of that place and time," there were "many *'ulama* of the Ogadenis and Qutbis and others." They followed al-Zayla'i and attached themselves to his *tariqa*.[25] Another *manqaba* (15) indicates that in spite of a severe famine that struck the Ogaadeen during Zayla'i's time there, he obtained a great deal of close support and continual help for his proselytizing from the Qutbi clan. When many of his students and adherents had left Kolonkol to search for food or had helped the resident population to drive their animals to better pastures, four men from the Qutbis stayed with their shaykh, one of them being Shaykh Abu Bakr bin Yusuf al-Qutbi,[26] Zayla'i's successor on his death in 1882, and the man designated by him to become the *Sahib al-Sajjada* or chief of the Qadiris in the Zayla'iya movement (*manqaba* 70).[27]

It seems likely that this Qutbi clan is the same as Lewis's Reer Sheikh Aw Qutub, a "priestly lineage," which is a branch of the Reer Fiqi 'Umar, whose special shrine is at Sheikh in northern Somalia.[28] No doubt attracted by Zayla'i's *baraka*, (charisma) four of the Qutbi *murids* (students) constantly helped the shaykh by assuming various duties, such as bringing him and the other students drinking and ablution water, or hunting game for food to be consumed by the group. Another had the task of cutting dates for Zayla'i. His eventual successor, Abu Bakr bin Yusuf al-Qutbi, was perpetually "in the Shaykh's presence and did not separate himself from him" (*manqaba* 15).[29]

It seems possible that the Qutbis (sometimes called Shaykhash or Shaykhal) believed they could renew their own *baraka* and prestige from associating with Zayla'i, and that he used them in his efforts to spread the Qadiri brotherhood, obviously an arrangement of mutual benefit.

For these reasons, it is not surprising that a large number of the *manaqib* included in the *Rahat al-Qalb* were related orally to the compiler, or sent him in writing, by members of the Shaykhal or Qutbi clan. (See Appendix for an effort to establish the genealogy of some of these Qutbi informants.)

There are various categories of *karamat* accomplished by Shaykh al-Zayla'i (during his lifetime and posthumously) and listed in the *Rahat al-Qalb*. Many of these concern food, often a problem in the famine-stricken Somali territories of the nineteenth century, as it is at present. Others show the shaykh's strong spiritual powers, curing the sick, impressing foreign learned men, being in two places simultaneously, reading his miracle-working poetry, etc.

In addition to the charitable contributions constantly being given to Shaykh Zayla'i and his followers, the master and his students had always to provide for themselves, whether at Kolonkol or elsewhere. One of the Qutbis ('Abdu b. Musa) served as cook for the group. His cuisine included dates of a special variety called *k.r.s.*[30] in Somali, to which was added meat from game or camel meat, honey, rice, and a kind of soup-like sauce or broth called *maraq* in Arabic. To this was added camel's milk when available. No doubt this diet was not very different from the food of other contemporary Somali nomads.[31]

Often, the Shaykh's *karamas* had to do with finding food for himself or his adherents. In *manqaba* 18, Zayla'i asks some travelers coming from the "high country" or Harar plateau (*barr*) for some of the thorn fruits (*Zizyphus spina*) which they brought with them; they were changed into delicious dates, quickly consumed by the entire group.[32] On another occasion, Zayla'i was visiting his friend Shaykh Ishaq Kal Lugh in the Rahanwiin District, who is buried at Darirsim near Bioley (or Biolay). Kal Lugh had nothing for breakfast, although he knew that Zayla'i was very fond of *aluh* (Somali for comb honey?). At that moment, Shaykh Ishaq chanced to look outside his hut and saw two men approaching with a large leather container of that kind of honey (*manqaba* 42).[33] At another time, Zayla'i reputedly fed nine of his students from a single sheep shoulder (*manqaba* 23).[34] Also, it is clear (*manqaba* 79) that the shaykh enjoyed his coffee. Being in the neighborhood of Harar, Zayla'i sent one of his Qutbi associates to fetch it from the town. Miraculously, the Shaykh's coffee container was full after a surprisingly brief interval, and Mu'allim 'Umar al-Qutbi was already back in the Shaykh's camp.[35]

On a more serious note, Shaykh Zayla'i was able to heal many illnesses, including smallpox. In the Shebelle District, a large town called B.s.l.h. was suffering from an epidemic of it. The Shaykh simply sent one of his students to this town and told him to shout as loudly as he could, "Smallpox, Shaykh Zayla'i tells you to leave the Shebelle District immediately." Instantly, claims the *Rahat al-Qalb*, those who were ill became cured "through the *baraka* of the Shaykh's prayer. And those who had left town because they were ill came back into it the same night, wholly well."[36] Similarly, three men suffering from tuberculosis (*al-sul*) came to the Shaykh, hoping to be cured. After praying for them, the Shaykh suddenly shouted, "Tuberculosis, leave these three men instantly." The three "vomited up blood and pus, and recovered in an instant through the permission of Almighty God, and were healed."[37] Zayla'i likewise had equal success with a blind man, who came to him, asking for his sight to be restored. Telling him to come back after prayers, Zayla'i "rubbed his eyes with his blessed hand, at which the blind man regained his sight imeediately, through the *baraka* of the Shaykh."[38]

It is worth noticing that Zayla'i, who made at least one pilgrimage to Mecca, had some remarkable experiences while in the Hijaz. He came to the attention of prominent persons through his learning, and he confounded those who were assumed to be—but were not—far more erudite than himself. Thus, as Zayla'i on one occasion was passing through Jidda on his way to Mecca, "a voice came to him which said, 'When you reach Mecca the Ennobled, the learned men of the *Haram* will ask you . . . questions on [Shafi'i] legal decisions, on religious duties, and on other legal matters'."[39] Reaching Mecca, Zayla'i went to the *Masjid al-Haram*, where a learned man was expounding the sciences to his students, so Zayla'i and his student (Muhammad ibn Nuh al-Qutbi) sat down in the class and listened for a short while. When the instructor asked the group extremely difficult questions on logic, Zayla'i was the only person able to answer despite the presence of many of the local 'ulama, who "swam in the sea of knowledge and drank daily from the Well of Zamzam." When the session ended, the teacher called Zayla'i up to him and asked him if he were "a jinn or a human being." A little while later, both Zayla'i and Muhammad ibn Nuh al-Qutbi were asked to answer further questions. Among the prominent questioners were Sayyid Ahmad ibn Zayni Dahlan, the Shafi'i mufti of Mecca, "and all of the questions were answered through the baraka of the Shaykh. . . ."[40]

One of Zayla'i's most surprising abilities was his power to hear the cries or prayers of those in trouble, even at great distances, and to help or rescue them. In one case, Zayla'i vanished momentarily from what he was doing; in another case, he went into an ecstatic state (jadhba). In the first case, the Rahat al-Qalb calls him "one of those who can take big steps" (ahl al-khatwa) as shown in manqaba 45:

. . . Zayla'i and his students were assembled in a [certain] spot . . . at the time of one of the five daily prayers. The Shaykh told one of the students to pray as imam for the group . . . and left the place of prayer. . . . Then he came back and his thawb (long shirt) was wet. . . . They were surprised at his departure and quick return, and at the wetness of his garment. One of the students touched the Shaykh's thawb at the end of the prayer and tasted it and found that the water was as salty as the sea, yet the sea was very far from where they were. They asked him about his departure and the water on his thawb, and he told them that a group of unfortunate persons were in their ship . . . "on the Sea of Berbera, and I went out to rescue them. I got to them and saved them from the sea; I left [you] for that reason. . . ."[41]

Another day, when Zayla'i and his followers were in Ethiopia, at a place called Lamashlindo,[42] and Zayla'i was, as usual, teaching the sciences, he suddenly went ecstatic and said, "God is most great," and put one hand on the top of his chest, "like a person praying" (*manqaba* 57):

> . . . He remained that way for a time. We were silent until he came to from his ecstatic state and opened his eyes as if he had awakened from sleep. He wiped off his hands as if they were damp, and the water ran off. We asked him about them being wet . . . and how he felt when he went ecstatic. He said that one of the women students (*murida*) had been taken by a crocodile in the Kinana River, but that he had wrenched her away. . . "She had cried out to me, 'Ya Shaykh 'Abd al-Rahman, save me.' I rescued her and freed her from the crocodile. . . ."[43]

The *manqaba* brings up some remarkable points: If Zayla'i was present in two places at once, was it his whole body, or merely his hands? Did he in fact simultaneously replicate himself? Here the *Rahat al-Qalb* offers no explanation, but leaves it to the reader to supply his own solutions. Another fact is that most Somali teaching, in Islamic sciences and many other matters, until quite recently was for men only. Lewis, in his *Pastoral Democracy*, makes this point; hence, it is surprising to read of Zayla'i's "women students (*muridat*)." Possibly this lady was a Galla or Oromo woman?

Lewis likewise points out how "shameful and dangerous" it is for anyone to steal the property of a shaykh. This point is made very forcibly in *manqaba* 48:

> . . . [The Shaykh] had a large camel, a special one . . . which carried his books and his ablution water when he wanted to go to a distant town, like Harar. . . . [Normally] the camel was in pasture under the Shaykh's protection; it was unharmed by jackals or lions or other wild beasts. One day the camel was feeding in a spot far from the Shaykh, when a gang of godless persons [*fassaq*] and robbers saw it. They wanted to kill it and eat its meat. . . .[44]

The *Rahat al-Qalb* reports that several of the gang were afraid to kill the animal, for they knew it belonged to Shaykh Zayla'i, and argued over it with the others. Finally, the man who most wanted to slaughter the animal produced a spear for the purpose, "as sharp as a knife." When he struck the camel's neck with it, he also cut deeply into his hand, and both the man and the camel died at once. At this, the others were surprised, but wasted no time in digging a grave:

> . . . but when they put him into it, as far down [as they could], the grave spat him out (*lafazahu*). They put him into the grave a second time, but it ejected him, and so on, seven times. After that, they went to the Shaykh . . . and acquainted him with the circumstances, and that not one of them had eaten the flesh of the camel, and sought the Shaykh's pardon. He said to them, "Eat the meat of the camel" and pardoned them and forgave the man who had killed it. And they put him back into his grave and the grave accepted him and did not reject him. . . . May God give us benefits through his [Zayla'i's] secrets and knowledge and grace. . . . Amin![45]

Other evidence of Zayla'i's remarkable powers arises from certain of his poems, *qasidas,* which possess a special rogatory or even "super-rogatory" power, like his "*Hadiyat al-Arwah,*" which Andrezejewski translates as "The Camel-Herder of Souls."[46] As Cerulli also points out, this poem, to many Somali Muslims, embodies stupendous spiritual force: It seems worth quoting this *karama* (33) in full:

> . . . Among his *karamas* is what I have been told by Shaykh 'Abdallah b. Mahmud al-Bakk'i al-Qadiri on the authority of Shaykh Muhammad b. 'Abdallah al-Tulbahanti (Dulbahante) al-Qadiri, a shaykh of the brotherhood in Aden, who had it from Shaykh 'Abdallah al-Mijertayni, a Qadiri shaykh at Berbera, from his Shaykh, Shaykh 'Abd al-Salam b. Hajj Jama', one of Zayla'i's students: an Ethiopian killed one of Zayla'i's *murids* by cutting his head off with a sword . . . they informed

the Shaykh that his student had died, killed [in that way]. The Shaykh got up and went with his followers to the place where the *murid's* body [lay], and said to the students, "Bring me the severed head." They brought it, and he placed it on its original spot on the neck. [Then] he chanted his famous verse from the *qasida Hadiyat al-Arwah:*

> Prophet of God, I have no Protector
> Save you, who guards me
> From severe torment . . .

[He chanted these lines] seven times, and the head rejoined the body in its [proper] place and the dead man stood up alive, with the permission of God. For that reason the *qasida* was called *Hadiyat al-Arwah.* This verse is included in it. It has many virtues and famous qualities. May God give us benefit through his *baraka* and knowledge. . . . Amin![47]

And this was not the end of the power of this most famous poem of Zayla'i's, for it helped convert a famous learned man, Shaykh 'Abdallah al-Hasani, to the Qadiriya. Until that time, according to the *Rahat al-Qalb,* al-Hasani had rejected all Sufi orders, but when he heard the following line from the *Hadiyat al-Arwah,* he took an *ijaza* from the Shaykh and joined the brotherhood:

> Zayla'i comes to you offering gifts
> Through them he bestows evidence
> Of his generosity. . . .[48]

Another frequent subject of Zayla'i's *manqabas* and miraculous acts was his ability to read other people's thoughts instantaneously. Thus several incidents involving his students show them thinking thoughts about their shaykh that were less than respectful. Zayla'i always makes some comment that shows them that he knows precisely what they are thinking, yet always forgives them. A variation (*manqaba* 43) shows a student wondering why Zayla'i does not lecture on the subject about which the student wants to hear. But, as soon as he thinks such a thought, the Shaykh turns from one topic to another, following his auditor's wishes, discussing in turn the *dhikr, hadiths,* and *tafsir.* Finally the Shaykh turned to the student and said, "May God protect you, Kulwayni," at which the embarrassed student sought Zayla'i's pardon.[49]

Certain other classifications of Zayla'i's *karamas* might be mentioned here: They show: (1) the full extent of his power over dangerous animals, (2) his role in proselytizing parts of Somalia, (3) his disdain for rulers (e.g., the Amir of Harar), and (4) miraculous events attributed to him after his death.

It appears that Zayla'i not only had power over crocodiles, having saved a woman from being attacked by one, but over lions (and undoubtedly other beasts) as well. One day, as Zayla'i was riding on horseback from Zayla' to Bulhar, accompanied by his pupil Shaykh 'Alam Zad al-Oghadeni and others, a lion rushed out and clamped its teeth on the tail of Zayla'i's horse. The Shaykh turned around and transfixed the lion "with the eye of exasperation." Immediately, the lion relaxed its hold and dropped to the ground, but before it struck the ground, it had time to say, "Glory to God, the Prophet and the Believers." When the lion recovered from its faint, Zayla'i got off his horse and struck it with his hand, telling it to "get up and go off on its business."[50]

The site of this episode, in northern and northwestern Somalia, points to a division of the entire country made by various Qadiri shaykhs, or perhaps even decided in Baghdad at the headquarters of the order. *Manqaba* 9 is of significance here, as it does not narrate any miraculous events, but rather outlines the territories assigned to Shaykh Zayla'i and two other Qadiri leaders, Hajj Sufi (died 1904) and Shaykh Uways of Brava (died 1909):

. . . The land [of Somalia] was divided for us, that is, the Qadiri community (*macshar*), from the Webi Shebelle to the land of Ethiopia and Berbera and what lies beyond it [was given] to Zayla'i. As for the ports (*banadir*) and what is beyond them, that was [given] to a man busy there at that time with teaching the external sciences (*al-'ulum al-zahira*). He was known as Shaykh 'Abd al-Rahman, called Hajj Sufi. As

for the remainder of the coastal region (*sawahil*) and the rest of the
Somali country, that was [given] to another man, Shaykh Uways b.
Muhammad al-Barawi, who came from Baghdad and had an absolute
wilaya over all of it. . . .[51]

The point was made above (page 14) that Zayla'i was accustomed to the
society of impoverished people, indeed that he preferred them to others, and
that his branch of the Qadiriya certainly had a populist tone about it. Thus
detail is illustrated in *manqaba* 31, in which Zayla'i and his students go to
Harar. They walk into the town and come to the gate of one of its mosques.
Zayla'i's students enter the mosque, where they find other students reading
Islamic sciences. Zayla'i gets into conversation with these students and
corrects their style of reading and their errors. The new students immediately
recognize Zayla'i as a man of immense learning, and eventually ask him to
write them a new grammar book (see page 17 above). However, among the
new group of students is the Sultan of Harar, Amir 'Abdallah bin Muhammad. At the end of one of Zayla'i's lectures, he came up to the Shaykh to ask
him a question. But Zayla'i was not afraid to give him a tongue-lashing,
saying:

> "Knowledge does not flow into a haughty man's heart. You were
> sitting in a place raised up above the other students when you were
> listening to my lecture." Now the Amir was humbled, and accepted
> the Shaykh's word and his advice . . . and sat down among the other
> students. . . .[52]

It is worth noticing that this incident could never have happened as told,
since Zayla'i was dead by 1882, and Amir 'Abdallah of Harar did not come
to the throne until 1885. Nevertheless, the anecdote clearly illustrates the
attitudes of Zayla'i and his adherents.

Another and final category of *karamat* were those worked by Shaykh
Zayla'i after his death. One of these is illustrated by the origin of the *Rahat
al-Qalb* itself, in which Zayla'i appeared in a dream to one of his followers.[53]

Others are associated with Zayla'i's tomb at Kolonkol. On one occasion, at Zayla'i's tomb, a group of seven shaykhs came together and started to do their Sufi *dhikr*. Several of them became ecstatic, and for some reason one man said, and repeated himself several times, "O Shaykh, you have abandoned us." Immediately, those present noticed a sudden stiff breeze which had sprung up. Several of the participants interpreted this as a significant sign, proving that the Shaykh was present among them, although he was not visible.[54]

On another occasion, after the Shaykh's death, three men were wandering in the desert near a place called Wadi al-Masha'ikh. They had been moving about at night for the space of three days but had found nothing to eat, nothing to drink. They were weak from exhaustion and lack of food and water. Then one of them made a *tawassul* to Shaykh Zayla'i, by reading aloud his *qasida* in *'ayn* ('Ayniya). Not long after that, when the three had arrived in a broad open space, they saw before them in the distance a large tree. So they decided to stop underneath it until they could either get some relief or die on that spot. To their surprise, once they reached the tree, they found under its branches a large table, covered with various foods, butter, milk with salt for the food. They ate greedily and satisfied themselves, and drank what they wanted. They continued on, and by the evening of that same day came to a place where there were some shepherds tending their animals. Then "they realized that they had been saved by reading the *Ayniya* in praise of the Prophet and by the *baraka* of Shaykh Zayla'i."[55]

Undoubtedly there are many more *manaqib* of Zayla'i still current that are not included in this collection. It would be worthwhile collecting them, since, as Andrezejewski says, they "throw light on many geographical, historical and social aspects of Somali life."[56]

Appendix

Many of the *manaqib* in the *Rahat al-Qalb* were supplied by those belonging to the Qutbi clan. It has seemed worthwhile to draw a tentative diagram of part of their lineage from the latter part of the nineteenth century into the

1950s. It is worth noticing that Zayla'i's successor (4) was the elder(?) brother of (5) 'Abdallah ibn Yusuf al-Qutbi, the compiler of the Qadiri book *Al-Majmu'at al-Mubaraka*. . . , first published in 1920. Shaykh 'Abdallah b. Yusuf was himself the author of the fourth section in this book, *"Nasr al-Muminin 'ala'l-maradat al-mulhidin*. . ." (*"Victory of the Believers Over the Defiance of the Heretics"*), a violent attack on the Salihiya.

Many other Qutbis are listed in the *Rahat*, about whom there is too little information to place accurately in the diagram.

The information below comes from the names of informants listed at the start of each *manqaba* in the *Rahat al-Qalb*.

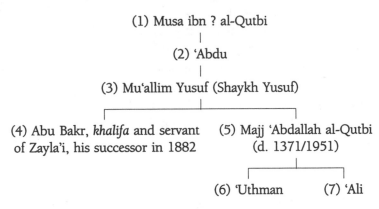

(1) Musa ibn ? al-Qutbi
|
(2) 'Abdu
|
(3) Mu'allim Yusuf (Shaykh Yusuf)

(4) Abu Bakr, *khalifa* and servant of Zayla'i, his successor in 1882

(5) Majj 'Abdallah al-Qutbi (d. 1371/1951)

(6) 'Uthman   (7) 'Ali

Notes

1. For the life and career of Muhammad b. 'Ali al-Shawkani, see Husayn b. 'Abdullah al-'Amri, *The Yemen in the 18th and 19th Centuries, a Political and Intellectual History*, London: Ithaca Press, 1985, Chapters 6–10.

2. I. M. Lewis, *Pastoral Democracy*. Oxford: 1961, p. 17, claims that in the seventeenth century Zayla' was a "dependency of the Sharifs of Mukha." It seems to have continued its links with Yaman as late as 1818, when the Zaydi Imam of Sana'a was still exiling political prisoners to Zayla' ('Amri, p. 90).

3. For an account of this episode, with a bibliography, see L. V. Cassanelli, *The Shaping of Somali Society*. Philadelphia: 1982, pp. 135–146.

4. 'Abd al-Rahman b. Shaykh 'Umar al-Qadiri, *Jala' al-'Aynanyn fi manaqib al-Shaykhayn al-Shaykh al-Wali Hajj Uways al-Qadiri wa'l-Shaykh al-Kamil al-Shaykh 'Abd al-Rahman al-Zayla'i*, Cairo, Matba'at al-Mashhad al-Husayni, ca. 1954. The *Rahat al-Qalb al-Mutawali' fi manaqib al-Shaykh 'Abd al-Rahman al-Zayla'i* is the second half of this book, on pp. 1–103.

5. *Rahat al-Qalb*, manqaba 1, pp. 2–4.

6. *Rahat*, manqaba 72, p. 40.

7. For the career of Ibrahim al-Rashid, see 'Ali Salih Karrar, *The Sufi Brotherhoods in the Sudan until 1900*, University of Bergen, Ph.D. dissertation, 1985, pp. 111 113 For the death of Zayla'i, the date is recorded in *Rahat*, pp. 4 and 57, where it is given in literal form in a *qasida* by 'Abd al-Rahman b. Shaykh 'Umar. Zayla'i's date of birth does not appear anywhere in this compilation. In another *qasida*, an *urjuza* by Zayla'i himself, called *Kanz al-Haqa'iq wa Sirr al-Daqa'iq*, about *tawassul* to various saints, Zayla'i mentions both Ahmad ibn Idris and his pupil Ibrahim al-Rashid (p. 53) as he enumerates his *silsila*:

> . . . To Shaykh Ahmad ibn Idris who
> Became for drinkers [of the truth]
> A fragrant intoxicant.
> And to Abu Salih the famous, his pupil al-Rashid
> Of blameless life. . .
> (lines 30–32)

Zayla'i apparently did not realize that Salih (of the Salihiya) was not Rashid's son, but his nephew, actually the son of his brother Muhammad wad-Sughayr (see the genealogical table of the Duwayhi clan in Karrar, p. 111).

8. A name related usually to a place of origin.

9. *Rahat*, p. 1.

10. *Ibid.*, p. 2.

11. *Ibid*, p. 45.

12. For *manqabas* 53 and 54, see pp. 30–31 in the *Rahat al-Qalb*. For *manqaba* 17, see p. 11, and for *manqaba* 75, see p. 41.

13. *Ibid*, p. 13.

14. *Ibid.* p. 30. For Zayla'i's troubles with the local *'ulama* of the Dasu at Gidle, see

pp. 30–31.

15. Shaykh or Hajj Sufi (Shaykh 'Abd al-Rahman b. Shaykh 'Abdallah al-Sha[n]shi al-Qadiri) died in 1322/1904, according to Qasim al-Barawi in his *Majmu'at Qasa'id fi madh Sayyid al-Anbiya'*. He was one of a series of prominent Somali Qadiri leaders, like Zayla'i, Isma'il al-Maqdashi, and Shaykh Uways. Supposedly Zayla'i attended Shaykh Sufi's *majlis* and his classes and was on close terms with him as a student, until he met Isma'il al-Maqdashi.

16. *Ibid.*, p. 5.

17. *Rahat*, p. 3. According to 'Ali Abdirahman Hersi, *The Arab Factor in Somali History*, UCLA Ph.D. dissertation, 1977, p. 253, Sayyid Hamza al-'Awsi inspired (third hand) the Zayla'iya movement, since he was himself inspired by teachers from Harar and Awsa. The beginnings of this phase of the Qadiriya in the early nineteenth century came there from Yaman, specifically from Zabid. The progress of this spiritual "dynasty" would then pass from Hamza al-'Awsi through Isma'il b. 'Umar al-Maqdashi to Zayla'i and on to the Qutbis. This topic is also discussed in Shaykh Ahmad Rirash, *Kashf al-Sudul Fi ta-rikh al-Sumal wa mamalikuhum al-sab'a*, Mogadishu 1974, a book to which I do not have access.

    The silsila of Hamza G. Mahmud al-'Awsi seems suspect, as it goes on to "Ifrah" or "Ifarah" and then to "Jund al-Rahman," then to Sayyid Abu Bakr b. 'Abdallah al-'Aydarus of Aden, who died in 1514! This information comes from 'Aydarus ibn al-Sharif 'Ali al-Nadiri al-'Alawi's *Bughyat al-Amal fi Tarikh al-Sumal*, Mogadishu 1374/1954, p. 226. These details are also confirmed (and the names vocalized) in a *qasida* by 'Umar al-Qadiri in the *Rahat al-Qalb*, where he gives his own *Silsila*, p. 47.

18. *Ibid.*, pp. 3–4.

19. The *Shatibiya* is a long poem on tajwid and Arabic grammar by Abu'l-Qasim al-Shatibi (538/1144–590/1194), called *Hirz al-Amani wa wajh al-Tahani*. It is one of the most "commented upon" books in Arabic, as more than 25 commentaries are known, according to I. Goldziher, *A Short History of Classical Arabic Literature*, Hildesheim 1966, p. 46.

20. If Zayla'i's poem, the *Hadiqat al-tasrif* (or "Garden of Conjugation") was published, it was probably before 1954, but the compiler gives no indication of where it appeared in print.

21. *Rahat*, p. 4.
22. See *Rahat*, p. 53, for the compiler's own poem praising Zayla'i, giving the date 1299 in literal form.
23. *Ibid.*, p. 4.
24. *Ibid.*, pp. 238–39.
25. *Ibid.*, p. 28.
26. *Ibid.*, pp. 9–10.
27. *Ibid.*, p. 39.
28. I. M. Lewis, *Pastoral Democracy*, p. 224 and note 2 on same page.
29. *Rahat*, pp. 9–10.
30. The actual vocalization of this Somali word is not clear.
31. *Ibid.*
32. *Ibid.*, pp. 11–12.
33. *Ibid.*, p. 23.
34. *Ibid.*, 13.
35. *Ibid.*, p. 43.
36. *Ibid.*, p. 40.
37. *Ibid.*, p. 41.
38. *Ibid.*
39. *Ibid.*, p. 14.
40. Ahmad ibn Zayni Dahlan, the Shafi'i *Mufti* of Mecca, appears in at least two *manaqib* in this book. He is often mentioned because he seemed to be (during the last third of the nineteenth century) a kind of *chef d'ecole* for conservative Shafi'is and those opposed to the ideas of Ibn Taymiya and the Wahhabis or neo-Wahhabis at the time. This antiradical personality was the author of a history of Mecca, and a book refuting Wahhabism and Wahhabi ideas, the *Durar al-Saniya fi'l-Radd 'ala'l-Wahhabiya*, a book still banned in Saudi Arabia because of its vituperative polemic attacks and cutting criticism of the Wahhabis. Dahlan was also on the side of those who used saintly mediation in prayer, like Zayla'i, Shaykh Uways, Hajj Sufi, and a majority of Muslim conservatives of this time and later. The poems and books written by him are known collectively as the *Dahlaniya*, especially when they are cited to reinforce conservative theological attitudes, as exemplified by Zayla'i and his followers, who particularly favored

tawassul, which was anathema to their opponents of the Salihi/Wahhabi school.

41. *Rahat,* p. 25.
42. Lamashlindo is a conjectural vocalization of the name of this Ethiopian town.
43. *Rahat,* p. 33.
44. Lewis, *Pastoral Democracy,* pp. 215–216. See pp. 26–27 in *Rahat* for *manqaba* 48.
45. *Rahat,* same reference.
46. See B. W. Andrzejewski, "The Veneration of Sufi saints and its impact on the oral literature of the Somali people and on their literature in Arabic," *African Studies,* XV, 1974, pp. 15–53. The author makes this point on p. 40 of his article.
47. *Rahat,* p. 19.
48. *Ibid.,* p. 19–20.
49. *Ibid.,* p. 23–24.
50. *Ibid.,* pp. 17–18.
51. *Ibid.,* p. 7.
52. *Ibid.,* p. 18–19.
53. *Ibid.,* p. 1.
54. *Ibid.,* pp. 34–35.
55. *Ibid.,* p. 35. This *qasida* in 'ayn is well known, and has much of the "rogatory power" of the *Hadiyat al-Arwah* ("*The Stimulator of Happiness*") and was written by Zayla'i when the Prophet appeared to him in a dream and asked him to write a poem of praise in his honor, of just 100 lines, as Zayla'i states in the fourth line from the end. This poem can be found in Qasim al-Barawi's *Majmuat al-Qasa'id,* pp. 46–63. Al-Barawi has turned it into a *takhmis,* with the first three hemistiches of every group of five added by himself.
56. Andrezjewski, "Veneration," p. 46.

CHAPTER TWO

The Sayyid and Saalihiya Tariga

Reformist, Anticolonial Hero

in Somalia

ABDUL S. BEMATH

THE MUSLIM RESPONSE IN AFRICA to colonialism and Christian influence was one effect of the resurgence of revivalist Muslim movements in the form of *tariqas* (brotherhoods). Thus, there were the rise of the Sudanese Mahdi and the Sammaniya *tariqa*, the resistance of 'Abd al-Qadir and the Qadiriya *tariqa* to French colonialism in Algeria and the Sanusiya of north Africa and its resistance to the French and Italians.

This study aims to outline the history of the anticolonial movement of religious leader Sayyid Muhammad 'Abdille Hasan (1899–1920). This rebellion was directed against Christian educational influence in Somalia as well as against European and Ethiopian imperial and expansionist encroachments in Somalia.

The Somalis were faced with threats to their land, economy and religion (Islam). The traditional Somali society was fragmented as it was beset with interclan rivalries for scarce resources, and clans were collaborating with the British and other imperial powers. The Muslim resistance to Ethiopian expansionism and colonial hegemony forged by the Sayyid into a united force nevertheless occurred in the midst of this clannish factionalism. Facilitating this was the Sayyid's military expertise, diplomatic skill, and ability to reconcile (and also exploit to his advantage) varying and conflicting clan differences, as well as the utilization of a Sufi religious *tariqa*, the Saalihiya, as an organizational and unifying base.

The Dervish wars have been extensively researched[1] and more emphasis will be placed here on Islam as a resistance ideology. The Sayyid's ideological and theological stance, the intellectual origins of his ideas and actions, and his utilization of the Saalihiya *tariqa* as an ideological and organizational base to Ethiopian expansionism and Euro-Christian imperialism will be briefly examined.

Ali A. Mazrui[2] divides early protests or responses to colonial rule into four categories: Protests of conservation, protests of restoration, protests of transformation, and protests of corrective censure. *Protests of conservation* involve those acts or movements that are aroused by a sense of impending peril to a system of values dear to the participants. This is a defensive reaction to conserve the system of values. *Protests of restoration* are nostalgic and seek to restore a past that has been disrupted or destroyed. *Protests of transformation* involve a profound disaffection with the existing system of values, rewards, and penalties, and aims at a radical change of the existing system. In Mazrui's fourth category, *protests of corrective censure*, the whole system of values, rewards, and penalties is unquestioned (as in the other categories of protests), but there is an ad hoc demand for a particular modification in the system. This may, for example, appear in the form of anger directed at a particular group of people, or a specific government policy or individual transgression.

Protests of conservation and of restoration are directed toward the preservation and the revival of the past, whilst protests of transformation are futuristically directed. The early colonial protests or protests of primary resistance have been either protests of conservation or of corrective censure.

Mazrui further identifies three psychological sources of protest, which may be cited as those of "anger," "fear," and "frustrated ambition." Anger and fear are emotional responses usually to external provocation. Frustrated ambition is an emotional drive directed to self-improvement, and this may be for material improvement, status, and greater prestige. Protests of restoration and of transformation are characterized by ambitious drive. In the former case the ambitious drive derives its sustenance from a deep nostalgia and aspiration to bring back what has passed away. Protests of transformation are innovative, and there is anger at the current state of affairs with the conviction that things can be changed. Fear is an essential factor in protests of conservation, whilst anger is a persistent source of corrective censure that can also include the elements of fear and even ambition. This study is an attempt to incorporate Mazrui's various insights into the Sayyid's early protests and resistance against colonial conquest.

The Sayyid's Early Life

Sayyid Muhammad was born on 7 April 1856, in the valley of Sa'madeeq, seven miles north of Buuhoodle water holes in the northeastern section of what was to become the British Somaliland protectorate. His father was a Bah Geri Ogaadeen Somali, and his mother was from the Dulbahante clan. He used these affinal links extensively in gaining recruits to the Dervish movement, thus illustrating the usage of traditional links in gaining support.

From the age of eight he was taught the Qur'an and the Shariah (Islamic law) by an Ogaadeen sheikh, and at age eleven had become a hafiz al-Qur'an (learned the Qur'an by heart). From a young age he showed qualities of leadership and horsemanship, which were essential to his resistance movement.[3] He also visited Kenya and Port Sudan where he is purported to have met the Mahdist general 'Uthman Digna. If this meeting did take place the Mahdist resistance must have inspired the Sayyid to lead a jihad (holy war) in Somalia. He travelled extensively, learning and preaching in search of Islamic knowledge in Harar, Mogadishu, and Nairobi.

In 1894 he went for the hajj (pilgrimage) to Mecca accompanied by thirteen fellow hajis. Here he met and was converted to the Saalihiya *tariqa* by its founder Muhammed Salih. This *tariqa* was gaining popularity in Arabia, and spreading across the Red Sea into East Africa. Muhammad Salih was a Sudanese of the Maliki school and from Dongola on the River Nile and must have exposed the Sayyid to the Mahdist revolt that had occurred a few years earlier. Mecca had also become the hub of the Muslim world; a meeting place for thousands of Muslims, it exposed the Sayyid to the Pan-Islamic ideas prevailing at that time.

The Various Tariqas

At that time a number of *tariqas* existed in Somalia and amongst these were the Dandarawiya, the Rifaiya, and the older and more important Ahmadiya and Qaadiriya *tariqas*. The Qaadiriya was older and founded by the Baghdadi saint Sayyid 'Abd al-Qadir Jilani (d. A.D. 1166), whilst the Ahmadiya and its offshoot the Saalihiya trace their ancestry to the great Meccan teacher and mystic Ahmad b. Idris al-Fassi (1760–1837).[4] Muhamad Salih was a close friend and pupil of al-Fassi and "was wholly in favor of reform and rejected traditional sufism; he was decidedly closer to the reforming Wahhabis than to the Qadiriya."[5] The Saalihiya *tariqa* was representative of a radically different neo-Sufi tradition, one that was opposed to the Qaadiriya in doctrine.

This was the era of the sheikhs in Somali history, and the Saalihiya *tariqa* gained many adherents. There was Muhammad Qulid al-Rashidi, who founded agricultural settlements along the upper valley of the Webi Shabeelle; Ismail ibn Ishaq al-Urwayni; and Sheikh 'Ali Nairobi. Among the Qaadiriya there was Sheikh Uways Mahaad or Muhammad, who founded the Uwaysiya in southern Somalia.

In traditional Somali society these sheikhs played a religious role and were called *wadaads*. They mediated between man and God, offered sacrifices, solemnized marriages, taught the Qur'an and offered prayers on behalf of the clan. Their settlements, called *jama'a* or *zawiya* were a welcome sanctuary to travellers and outcasts, and the formative bonds forged here transcended divisions of clans and kinship. In contrast to the *wadaads*, there were the *warrenleh* (spear-bearers) or secular men more concerned with the solving of secular problems. During the 1890s and after, these *wadaads* increasingly became involved in the affairs of the world and, according to Samatar, "acted as heads of religious brotherhoods, and their involvement in secular affairs ranged from indirect influence over clan leaders like Dandarawi and Zayli'i in the Ogaadeen to acquisition of actual political power like Muhammad 'Abdille Hasan."[6]

Somalia at the Time of the Sayyid

During the last quarter of the nineteenth century, Islam arose with a new vitality and dynamism amongst the Somalis. The annual flow of *hajis* to Mecca tripled and the brotherhoods prolifitated with religious centers (*jama'a*) dotting the Somali peninsula. In Somalia, there was a renewed immigration of Arab sheikhs and *fiqih* jurists who built mosques and opened up theological schools and centers of learning with emphasis on the teaching of the Shariah.[7]

There were various influential factors involved in this resurgence of Islam, among them the subjugation of Muslims and Muslim lands to Euro-Christian rule; e.g., Britain's seizure of Egypt in 1884 and the French conquest of North Africa and Algeria. Along the east coast of Africa, the Omani sultan of Zanzibar had been subjugated by European hegemony and the same applied to Asian Muslims.

In Somalia there was increasing militancy and xenophobia to Europeans, as illustrated in the case of F.L. James, who at the *tariqa* settlement of Faf, was met with antagonism. His Somali helpers were scorned for helping *kaffirs* (infidels) and were considered no better than *kaffirs* themselves. In contrast to this, three years earlier in 1883, British explorer Captain H. Swayne found these sheikhs the traveller's best friend and considered them to be helpful, intelligent, and useful in giving introductions and passing a traveller from tribe to tribe.[8] The killing of Sudanese Muslims by the British during the Mahdist revolt also contributed to the Somalis' antipathy toward Europeans and Christians.

The Somalis were not only threatened by the Euro-Christians but also by the famine-stricken Ethiopian Christians whose armed bands were expanding eastwards into the Somali Ogaadeen in search of grazing land and driven by a desire to conquer Somali territory in a bid to participate in the "scramble for Africa" by the various European powers. Various *tariqa* settlements belonging to both the Qaadiriya and the Ahmidiya were threatened and looted, and "the ancient *Tariqa* colony at Qulunqul and the tomb of the founding saint of Qaadiriya's northern branch, 'Abd ar-Rahman az-Zeyli'i, lay in ruins 'sacked by the Ethiopians.'"[9] The Somalis felt threatened by Christian invaders, whether these be the Ethiopians or the European powers such as the British or Italians.

The Return of the Sayyid to Somalia

Thus, at the time of the return of the Sayyid to Somalia from Mecca there existed a marked antagonism to Europeans, Christians, and Ethiopians. the Muslim world was in tumult, and there was a resurgence of Pan-Islamic ideals, the emergence of various *tariqas* and a more puritanical form of Islam. The various religious *wadaads* were now forced by these circumstances and influences to play a more secular and political role in contrast to their traditional one dealing with spiritual matters. The Sayyid could utilize these fears and grievances in building support against the Ethiopians, the British, and the Italians.

The Sayyid's resistance had a strong religious underpinning, and this legitimized his leadership while his political oratory served as a practical tool in exercising this leadership.[10] His ideological stance was influenced by the various experiences and exposures he had in Mecca, the Mahdist revolt and the Pan-Islamic feelings of that era. In conjunction with this were a number of incidents that occurred on his return to Somalia; these included the alleged killing of a *Mu'addhin* (prayer caller) who had disturbed a British governor's sleep during the call to prayer. There was also another incident when a British customs official insisted that the Sayyid pay customs dues and unceremoniously riffled the baggage of the newly arrived pilgrim. The Sayyid answered, "Did you pay customs dues when you landed here? Who gave you permission to enter our country?"[11] The incident had a profound effect on him, arousing his antipathy and anticolonial attitudes, illustrating Mazrui's psychological aspect of anger as a motivating factor in protest against colonial rule and foreign intrusion. This anger was further intensified when he met a group of Muslim children on his way from Berbera to his Dulbahante kinsmen. These Muslim orphans attended a Catholic mission at Daymoole, and, on being asked to state their clan affiliation (the surest way to denote Somali identity), they replied that they "belonged to the clan of the fathers."[12] On another occasion he was outraged when a Muslim boy replied that his name was "John Abdullah." This was the anger of the indigenous intelligentsia against cultural assimilation by Europeans via mission schools, and more significant in this case as the Sayyid came from an opposing Islamic school of learning and tradition, a tradition that was strong both orally and in writing, and not dominated by Western thoughts and values. This Christian "invasion" and European intrusion intensified his ideological warfare against foreigners and his utilization of Islam as a resistance ideology.

Mazrui's category of fear as a motivating force can be seen here. The advance into the Ogaadeen of Ethiopian hordes, pillaging and burning indiscriminately truly alarmed the Somalis. The wholesale sack and destruction of the holy tariqas, regarded as sacrosanct in Somali eyes—and therefore exempt from any physical harm—especially horrified the Somalis. The Sayyid could capitalize on this fear by the Somalis, who were in the pathway of these invading forces, and he exploited it well in gaining support for his Dervish cause.

This is a case of the protest of conservation coupled with the psychological aspects of fear and anger in protest movements. The protest of conservation and anger was exemplified in the Sayyid's message to his inland countrymen bearing the scourge of the invading Ethiopians in the following message:

In the name of God the Beneficent, the Merciful . . . Infidel invaders have come to surround us. They have come to corrupt our ancient religion, to settle our land, to seize our herds, to burn our qaryas (villages), and to make our children their children. . . . Not too long ago you heard how the Amhaar fell on the Reer Amaadin (clan name) and carried off many of their camels in loot. If you follow me, with the help of God, I will deliver you from the Amhaar.[13]

He also acquired support from the *jama'a* inhabitants, especially those along the Tug Fafan who feared the Ethiopian advance. The Saalihiya *tariqa* could expand and override clan and tribal differences, demonstrating the cohesiveness and integrative character of these *jama'as* during crisis situations. The Sayyid cleverly utilized the Saalihiya *tariqa* as an ideological and organizational base.

The Sayyid's Use of the Saalihiya Tariqa

How was the Saalihiya *tariqa* utilized as a Muslim resistance ideology and organizational base by the Sayyid? What social, religious, and political structures existed that facilitated the utilization of this *tariqa* as a tool of resistance?

The Sufi *tariqas* could cut across lineages, kinship groups, classes, and therefore play an integrative role. The traditional Somali society is egalitarian, and there is no centralized form of authority; kinship was the key to the traditional Somali political organization. The Sufi *tariqas* are not inherently political by nature, but because they possess a centralized hierarchical tendency, they could be (and were) used to cut across tribal and clan differences to make a united force. This is precisely what the Sayyid had done with the Saalihiya.

Upon arrival in Berbera the Sayyid started propagating the message of the Saalihiya. As a *tariqa* with a puritanical and militant message, the Saalihiya was vehemently opposed to the more doctrinally relaxed Qaadiriya. The Sayyid accused the latter of moral laxity and *bidat* (undesirable innovation) practices, among these were the chewing of *qaat* (a mild narcotic)—a habit the Qaadiriya indulged in during *dhikr* (Sufi ritual dance)—smoking, excessive indulgence in luxuries, tea, coffee, and wearing infidel clothing. He also sharply attacked their practice of *tawasul* (intercession of saints for believers with God). The ritual of *tawasul* was accepted by the Berbera Qadiris, who encouraged pilgrimages to neighborhood tombs, and the Sayyid frequently charged that this was a heresy.[14]

The Sayyid also preached that his master Muhammad Salih was the preeminent saint of his time and that the Qaadiriya should abandon their sect for the Saalihiya. This incensed the Qadiriya, who denounced him as an excited, misguided upstart. In addition, he confronted various *'ulama* (men learned in religious law) such as Sheikh Madar, Aw Gaas Muhammad, and his former teacher 'Abdillaahi 'Aruusi. They warned him that he was transgressing the way of Islam. But they also warned the British vice-consul that the Sayyid was a hindrance to the future stability of the fledgling, newly established protectorate. However, captain H.E.S. Cordeax took no action against him, even though Aw Gaas Muhammad pointedly told him that the Sayyid was brewing up something. "If you do not arrest him now," he reportedly told the British official, "you will go very far to get him."[15] Prophetic words indeed. The Qaadiriya finally persuaded the vice-consul to close down the Saalihiya mosque in Berbera.

The leaders and followers of the Qaadiriya *tariqa* were involved in the British protectorate administration and had a vested economic interest to maintain. The British consul Colonel J. Hayes Sadler cultivated friendship with the local *'ulama* such as Sheikh Madar and Aw Gaas.[16] A healthy economy and administration were beginning to emerge, and the Qaadiriya were disinclined to disrupt this by following the Sayyid's anti-European preachings. And the elders constituted part of a small but growing administrative and economic bourgeoisie. This falls under the category of the protest of conservation and corrective censure, a censure against the *bidat* practices of the Qaadiriya, mentioned earlier. He skillfully (perhaps cynically) fulminated wrathfully against Qaadiraya's collaboration with the colonial order, a circumstance that played up to terrific effect the Somalis' natural xenophobia towards outsiders.

The Doctrinal Differences Between the Saalihiya and Qaadiriya Tariqas

The Saalihiya *tariqa* came from a radical neo-Sufi tradition, one that was opposed to the Qaadiriya in doctrinal matters. A host of doctrinal differences between the various schools of Islamic mysticism existed, such as the Wahhabi-influenced cluster of neo-Sufists (Ahmadiya, Sanusiya, Tijaniya) as opposed to classical Sufism (Qaadiriya-related) in the rise of the Sayyid and Muslim resistance.[17] The Qaadiriya scholars such as Sheikh Uways b. Muhammad and Sheikh Qasim al-Barawi wrote little in contrast to the northern Somali polemicist Sheikh 'Abdallah ibn Mu'allim Yusuf al-Qutbi of Kolonkol, who wrote extensively and bitterly against the Saalihiya *tariqa*. In al-Qutbi's five-piece collection *al-majmu'at al-mubaraka (The Blessed Collection)*, Saalihiya, Wahhabis, and even the Taymiya are attacked by name.[18]

One of the pieces in the collection entitled "Victory of the Believers" attacked the Saalihiya as a den of heretics bent on thwarting true faith. From Kharijite theology, the Saalihiya seem to have taken the position that an attack on the lives or possessions of other Muslims who do not adhere to their views was lawful. The Sayyid, in his "*Risala*" piece, for example, justified his attack on Muslims who aided and kept company with unbelievers. Those Muslims who did not readily profess to the Muslim faith, who did not observe the Friday prayer and who abandoned the Muslim Community should be stigmatized as unbelievers, he claimed.[19]

Muslims who wore infidel clothing, walked like unbelievers, or participated in their gatherings or festivals, could be, he held ferociously, branded infidels themselves. The Sayyid loved quoting a saying of the Prophet: "Whoever resembles a certain people, is, in fact, one of them." From the Wahhabis, moreover, he took the notion that pilgrimage and visits to the tombs of dead saints should be prohibited, and this fed well into his general abhorrence of any sort of *tawasul*. Diametrically opposed to the Sayyid, al-Qutbi, the Qadiri, claimed that arguments could be made for the practice of *tawasul*. Al-Qutbi viewed the Saalihiya as fundamentally anti-intellectual in hindering the reading of devotional books and the law texts of the various schools. The Sayyid countered the charge by accusing Qaadiriya of idolatrous innovation. In turn, al-Qutbi claimed the Saalihiya had adopted from the Shi'its the "erroneous" distinction between dead and live saints. Sheikh al-Qutbi further argued that there, in fact, existed no difference between *tawasul* to the Prophet himself and *tawasul* through subordinate intermediaries for similar purposes. By objecting to the doctrine of saintly intercession with God for the benefit of the living, the Saalihiya were, al-Qutbi complained, interfering with a fundamental Muslim duty of pilgrimage. Al-Qutibi went on to declaim, rather provocatively, that the deceased saint had a special sort of existence between life an death and that his spiritual powers remained unimpaired. Therefore, according to Al-Qutbi, there was no difference, so far as their intercessory powers were concerned, between a living and a dead saint, contrary to the teachings of the Saalihiya, Wahhabis and their spiritual ancestor, Ibn Taymiya.

Muhammad Salih, al-Qutbi continued in his bitter attack, could not be viewed as the "spiritual pole" or the "great intermediary" of his age, nor as a descendant of the house of the Prophets; neither did men of religion speak favorably of him, nor could he be regarded as a *"mujtahid"*, or an independent interpreter of the laws or Shari'a. To bolster his position, al-Qutbi cited as an authority the famous jurist and theologian al-Suyuti (died 1504), who held that the gates of independent legal innovation had been closed about 500 years ago. Hence, anybody who claimed to be a *mujtahid* was suspect and to be condemned. He derided the Saalihiya *tariqa* as heretical, deceptive, and satanic—a pharaohic outfit.

Al-Qutbi defended tobacco smoking, coffee drinking, the use of qaat (*catha edulis*, a mild narcotic to which many Somalis and Harraris are addicted)—these being unrecommended but not actually forbidden; he praised coffee as the "fruit of saints." Dancing by Sufis, as dancing at festivities and weddings, was acceptable, al-Qutbi held, so long as the motive remained pure.[20] Thus, there were these (and many other) doctrinal differences between the two *tariqas* and, as usual in such sectarian struggles, the members of each *tariqa* questioned the legitimacy of the other's beliefs.

As to the role the Sayyid's intellectual development played in the Muslim resistance to Christian encroachment, this was closely tied to the doctrinal differences between the two *tariqas*. Furthermore, the Sufism that he inherited had an influence on his intellectual thinking and development. The Sayyid was shaped by a kind of reformed mysticism that sprang out of a general Muslim revival in the form of reformist brotherhoods influenced by the puritanical doctrines of the Arabian Wahhabis. The neo-Sufis were stricter, more literal in their interpretation of the faith; by contrast Qaadiri Sufis adhered to a broader, and on occasion more allegorical, interpretation of the Qur'an and the traditions. The neo-Sufis were also more militant and tended to call for a literal return to the basics of the Shari'a—thus typifying the protests of conservation and corrective censure, as also the protests of transformation. These wanted a radical change in society.

This neo-Sufi puritanical attitude was reflected in his intellectual thoughts and writings as, for example, the Sayyid's *Risala* (of which more shortly) clearly demonstrates. The Sayyid was, moreover, a master of political oratory and used this as a form of 'public persuasion': in inspiring the faithful and denouncing the foe. This, coupled with his religious zeal, played a decisive role in forging the various conflicting clans into a united fighting force.

In his "*Risala al-Biyamaal*" ("Message to the Biyamaal clan") and in "*Qam'i al-Mu'anidin*" ("Suppression of the Rebellious"), one gets an indication of his intellectual resources and his significance as a political and religious leader. The "*Qami'i*" stands as a monumental apologia to Muhammad Salih (the Somali leader's spiritual mentor) as well as to Salih's letter which practically excommunicated the Sayyid. Commenting on the spiritual state of the Somalis, the Sayyid questions whether their beliefs were such that they could still be considered Muslim; he also defines the enemy and those who maintained relations with infidels. He hotly refuted here a denunciation of him by one Mahumad b. Yusuf al-Warsanghali, as well as justified his actions in order to clear his name from his master's accusatory letter.

The Sayyid further elaborated on his political ideas. As an admirer of Muhammad ibn 'Abd al-Wahhab and a student of the neo-Hanbali thinker Ibn Taymiya, the Sayyid spoke of the "order of the world" (*nizam al-'alam*) maintained by "governors, walis, and sultans," and characteristically inveighed against it as a world of sin and idolatry. He also claimed, as was common among Somalis of his religious training and disposition, a Hashemi descent from the Prophet's family. The *Risala* provides more insights into his intellectual thinking. In it he praised the Biyamaal for resisting the Italians. He also clarified here certain doctrinal points and answered criticism made by those who opposed the *jihad* (holy war). The *jihad* was now, he argued, an inescapable Muslim duty in view of the fact that Muslims and Muslim lands had been tyrannized and brutalized by Christian invaders. He went on at length to dwell on various kinds of *jihads*—e.g., the *jihad* against unbelievers, the great *jihad* against those who held the opinion that Christians had brought peace and prosperity to the land—a direct allusion to the *'ulama* of Berbera who had, so to speak, run him out of town. The Sayyid branded Christians invaders, who remained fundamentally hostile to Muslims. Peace and prosperity could emanate only from God, the Qur'an and the sunnah (the words and actions of the prophet Muhammad.) The Sayyid again severely criticized Muslims who maintained Christians as friends and collaborated with them. Muslims, he declared rather ominously, who associated with Christians should be subject to attack and should be shunned by other Muslims. The reference related to Muslims who served as guides to the Europeans, meaning the Somalis involved in the British Protectorate administration and the clans that now had vested interests to maintain under British protection.

In summary, had it not been for the presence of the French, British, Italians, and the Ethiopians, who were seen as common enemies by the Somalis, this religious and doctrinal dispute might have created a large scale religious rift between the two *tariqas*. In view of the deep doctrinal antagonism between the two *tariqas*—and the consequent ill feeling generated among their devotees—it is a wonder that the Somalis in the closing decades of the twentieth century were not plunged into a disastrous internecine blood letting based on religious discord, and possibly civil war.

Notes

1. See Douglas Jardine. *The Mullah of Somaliland.* London: Herbert Jenkins, 1923.

I. M. Lewis, *The Modern History of Somaliland: From Nation to State*. London: Weindenfeld & Nicolson, 1965. R. L. Hess, "The poor man of God-Muhammad Abdullah Hassan." in N. R. Bennett, ed. *Leadership in Eastern Africa: Six Political Biographies*. Boston: Boston University press, 1968, pp. 65–108. In my B.A. honors thesis (unpublished: University of South Africa, 1980), I mentioned these wars. I dealt with varying perspectives on rebellions and tried to show some discerning features of the "Scramble for Africa" rebellions. Then I gained theoretical insights into rebellions/revolts with respect to causes, leadership and organization of rebellions from various sources. I utilized these in the Sayyid's rebellion, and finally gave information on leadership and organization of his Dervish movement. Also I put the rebellion in a relative deprivation perspective. A shortened version of this dissertation bearing the same title: "*Sayyid Muhammad Abdullah Hassan and the Somali Rebellion: 1899–1920*" appears in *al-'ilm* (*Journal of the Centre for Research in Islamic Studies*), Vol. 4, Rabi 'al-Awwal 1401=January 1984; University of Durban-Westville, Durban, S. Africa.

2. Ali a. Mazrui, "Postlude: Toward a Theory of Protest" is edited by A. A. Mazrui and R. I. Rotberg and in *Protest and Power in Black Africa*. New York: OUP, 1970, pp. 1185–1196.

3. S. S. Samatar, *Oral Poetry and Somali Nationalism: The Case of Sayyid Muhammad 'Abdille Hasan*, Cambridge: Cambridge University Press, 1982, p. 102.

4. Samatar, *Oral Poetry*, p. 96.

5. B. G. Martin, *Muslim Brotherhoods in Nineteenth Century Africa*. Cambridge: Cambridge University Press, 1976, p. 179.

6. Samatar, *Oral Poetry*, p. 97.

7. *Ibid.*, p. 93.

8. R. L. Hess, "The Poor Man of God—Muhammad Abdullah Hassan," p. 74.

9. Samatar, *Oral Poetry* p. 96.

10. Hess, "The Poor Man," p. 93.

11. Martin, *Muslim Brotherhoods*, p. 181.

12. Samatar, *Oral Poetry*, p. 107.

13. *Ibid.*, p. 112.

14. Martin, *Muslim Brotherhoods*, p. 181.

15. Samatar, *Oral Poetry*, p. 107.

16. *Ibid.*, p. 106. Aw Gaas was the chief Islamic magistrate.
17. Samatar, *Oral Poetry*, pp. 185–186. Martin, *Muslim Brotherhoods*, pp. 177–179.
18. Martin, *Muslim Brotherhood*, pp. 199–201.
19. *Ibid.*, p. 197.
20. *Ibid.*, p. 200 and p. 237.

CHAPTER THREE

Sheikh Uways Muhammad of Baraawe, 1847–1909

Mystic and Reformer in East Africa

SAID S. SAMATAR

IN ASSESSING RECENT SCHOLARSHIP of Somali studies, one is struck by the contrast in academic attention devoted to the two great religio-political movements led respectively by Sayyid Muhammad 'Abdille Hasan and Sheikh Uways Muhammad at the beginning of this century.[1] While the Sayyid and the Somali Dervishes have been made the object of massive public and private veneration in Somali circles for their contribution to the growth of Somali nationalism, the Uwaysi movement has scarcely occasioned a whisper of academic interest or national recognition. The poverty of academic attention given to the Uwaysiya is the more curious in view of the movement's considerable impact on East African Islam at the turn of the century and its continuing vitality for millions of devotees in the region today.

To be sure, the history of the Uwaysi Sufis does not afford students of Somali studies the dazzling record of political drama and nationalistic appeal that characterizes the Dervish movement. Yet, if their political achievement has been less dramatic, the Uwaysi Sufis may well have outshone the Dervishes in religious influence. There is therefore, in the opinion of this writer, an urgent need to examine and bring out the place of the Uwaysi brotherhood in Somali religious life. This study attempts to make a modest start towards this objective.

Islamic Revivalism in Northeast Africa

In a preliminary discussion of the origins and growth of the Uwaysi movement, perhaps the place to begin is with late nineteenth-century Islamic revivalism in northeast Africa, a revivalism of which the Uwaysiya movement seems to have been one manifestation. In the last quarter of the nineteenth century, Eastern African Islam experienced a widespread religious reawakening. During this period, Islam emerged with renewed vitality and fervor among its Somali devotees. Brotherhoods proliferated with religious centers (jama'a) dotting the Somali hinterlands and the East African coast from Zayla' to Zanzibar. The annual flow of Somali pilgrims to and from Mecca tripled.[2] The period also saw a renewed immigration into Somalia of Arab sheikhs and faqihs who built mosques and opened up theological schools and centers of learning where the teaching of the Shari'a and of other forms of sacred law were reemphasized. The outburst of zealous Islam in East Africa seems to have been part of a wider religious revival in the Muslim world. The recrudescence of militant Islam in Africa and Asia is said to have been the outcome of the increasing subjugation of Muslims and Muslim lands to Euro-Christian rule.[3] In the eyes of the Muslim faithful, this had been throughout the nineteenth century a disquieting trend that finally acquired a painful climax in its closing years.

In Egypt, ever since Napoleon routed the last of the Mamluks at the Battle of the Pyramids in the 1790s, European encroachment had continued to grow apace. It culminated in Britain's seizure of Egypt in 1884. The French had begun the conquest of North Africa with Algeria in the 1830s and had completed it with the annexation of Tunisia and Morocco in succeeding years. In Muslim West Africa, too, French colonial expansion was at work, staking out vast dominions in two decades (1880–1900). On the East African coast, the Omani sultans of Zanzibar had been reduced to impotence by half a century of European hegemony. As early as 1844 the British Consul's authority on the coast was so overwhelming that the frequent succession disputants to the throne sought to enlist the aid of the "power behind the throne."[4] In the succeeding decades, the power and influence of Europe over Zanzibari affairs continued to increase. In 1886 the aging Said Bargash was forced to sign a humiliating Anglo-German treaty of delimitation, which, in a high-handed fashion, stripped the sultan of sovereignty over his East African dominions except for a few coastal towns and their immediate hinterlands.[5]

The fortunes of Muslim Asia were hardly better off. Here, the Sultan of the Ottomans, symbol of Muslim sovereignty and the embodiment of its spiritual integrity, had for long been ridiculed as the "sick man of Europe,"[6] while his rickety empire continued to crumble under the corrosive activities of European diplomats, and traders, and concession-seekers. Pressed for political reform, forced to borrow loans at extortionate rates of interest, plagued by foreign-inspired sedition and discord among their Christian subjects, and threatened with invasion from without, the Ottomans lived from crisis to crisis in the last quarter of the nineteenth century.[7]

The shock and humiliation of defeat could not but entail a traumatic impact upon the Muslim community, a community that entertains a lofty image of itself, as the "noblest of mankind"[8] and the embodiment of divine expression.[9] Muslim response to the imposition of Christian rule was varied, however, ranging from a thorough breakdown of the traditional system and the concomitant rise of a secular state on the European model (as in the case of the Ottomans) to the militant retrenchment of puritanical Islam, as illustrated by the Wahhabi state in Arabia.

With respect to African Islam, a widespread response seems to have involved the rise of the "reformist movement." The resurgence of revivalist movements in Muslim Africa was first studied by J.S. Trimingham[10] and later, quite ably, by B.G. Martin.[11] At the heart of each of these reform movements lay a Sufi brotherhood led by a charismatic figure, a sort of John the Baptist, who called men and women to repentance and sought to restructure society by rededicating it to the worship of its creator and to conformance with his sacred laws. Concomitant with the rise of the charismatic was the popularization of the millennialist doctrine.[12] The Sudanese *Mahdia* also typified this spirit of millennialism, but traits of it can also be detected in the Somali (*saalihi*) Dervishes and the Sanusis of Libya. The socio-political dislocations resulting from European intervention were, in the words of Martin, seen in "religious colors, as part of an ongoing struggle between Christian intruders and the Islamic polity."[13] Furthermore, these movements tended to attribute the erosion of the Muslim position vis-a-vis the Christians to divine displeasure, i.e. Muslims were allowed to suffer under the Christian infidel because they were under divine disfavor owing to their sinful ways and departure from the "straight path."[14] The way to regain favor with God was, therefore, to govern society in strict accordance with His laws.

The revivalist spirit in Islam swept Somalia from the 1890s onwards. Of the dozen or so orders that operated in Somalia from the 1890s onwards, two were exceptionally important: the Qaadiriya and the Ahmadiya brotherhoods. The Qaadiriya *Tariqa* (*turuq*, pl.) or path was founded by the Baghdadi saint Sayyid 'Abdul-Qaadir al-Jilani (died A.D. 1166), while the Ahmadiya and its off-shoot, the Saalihiya, trace their ancestry to the great Meccan teacher and mystic Ahmad b. Idris al-Fasi (1760–1837). Being older and more established, the Qaadiriya order commanded greater membership among the Somalis but was less puritanical than Ahmadiya. Locally, the Qaadiriya brotherhood is split into two "powerful" branches. In the north, the Zayli'iya, named for Sheikh 'Abdul-Rahman Zayli'i who died in 1882, is more influential; while in the south, the Uwaysiya founded by Uways Muhammad tends to predominate.

The Emergence of the Uwaysiya Brotherhood

Documentary evidence on Sheikh Uways and the Uwaysiya mainly comes from *Jala' al-Aynayn fi Manaqib al-Shaykhayn al-Shaykh al-Wali Hajj Uways al-*

Qadiri wal-Shaykh 'Abdul-Rahman al-Zayli'i, and *Jawhar al-Nafis fi Khawwas al-Sahykh Uways*, two hagiographies authored by 'Abdul-Rahman b. 'Umar al-Qadiri.[15] Ethnically, Uways appears to have been a Black Tunni. Although the Black Tunni clan live as rural cultivators and pastoralists (as opposed to their urbanized kinsmen, the White Tunni), Uways seems to have belonged to an urban, well-to-do family. Born (April 1847) and raised in the town of Baraawe, he was the son of a minor religious notable, named al-Hajj Muhammad b. Bashiir and his mother was Fatima b. Bahro. Although little is known of his childhood and adolescence, the young Uways studied the Qur'an, Qur'anic exegesis, and other religious sciences with one Sheikh Muhammad Tayini (or Zayini) al-Shashi (also pronounced al-Shanshi). Impressed by the young man's intelligence and pious disposition, Muhammad Tayini introduced him to the esoteric teachings of the Qaadiriya and encouraged him to travel to Baghdad, spiritual fountain of the Qaadiriya and a principal center of theological studies. For some time before leaving for Baghdad to study the "Sufi Way," Uways tarried in Baraawe, withdrawing to an old mosque on a coral reef where he is alleged to have cured victims afflicted by *jinn* (or devils).

In 1870 Uways left for Baghdad, and in the next ten years undertook a peripatetic learning in the Middle East, making a series of pilgrimages to Mecca and other holy places of Islam. In Baghdad uways studied with the reigning divine of the Qaadiriya Sayyid Mustafa b. Salman al-Jilani. Eventually, Uways received, or claimed to have received, the *ijaza* (authorization to preach on behalf of the order similar to Christian ordination) from his 'Iraqqi master, who delegated him to serve as Qaadiriya's spiritual envoy in Somalia and possibly East Africa.[16]

In 1880 Sheikh Uways returned to Baraawe by way of the Hejaz, Yemen, and northern Somalia. In norther Somalia in 1883, he allegedly stopped at the tomb of the recently deceased Sheikh 'Abdul-Rahman al-Zayli'i near Qulunqul in the Haud to pay him homage and to receive from him a symbolic *ijaza* to preach and ordain new deputies (khaliifas). Zayli'i had been a revered Qaadiriya saint, and Uways's symbolic visit to honor him proved to be helpful in establishing his credibility as the spiritual successor to the renowned Zayli'i. Subsequently, this enabled Uways to bolster his position against his many detractors. At Baraawe, Uways used his charismatic powers and spiritual prestige to gain leadership of the Qaadiriya in southern Somalia, which soon assumed the name of Uwaysiya.[17]

But Uways' career in southern Somalia was not without difficulties. His hagiographer speaks of the "envious" who lost no opportunity in "defaming" the name of the saint. B.G. Martin speculates that the "envious" were the rival brotherhoods of Ahmadiya and Saalihiya, but in fact oral testimony hints that the "envious" came from closer quarters—from members of Uways' own household, in particular an elder uncle who resented Uways's rising influence and denounced him as a "charlatan" and "upstart" (*wadaad kitaab gaab*).[18] In time the Bravanese opposition to the Sheikh became so intense that he decided to quit the Somali coast. In about 1898–9 he left for the interior, where he founded a flourishing agricultural town 50 miles inland, which he christened, significantly, the "Town of Peace" (Beled al-Amin).

At Beled al-Amin, Uways's missionizing efforts were rewarded with impressive successes. Nomad and farmer flocked to his community, bringing with them gifts in vast amounts of livestock and farm produce. The material gifts brought by the new converts freed the sheikh and his numerous deputies to devote their time and energy fully to spreading the influence of their order. With messianic zeal, they sallied forth from Beled al-Amin to take the banner of Uwaysiya to the Abgaal, Geledi, Magani, and Shiidle clans in Benaadir province, the riverine cultivators in Lower Jubba and the Upper Jubba.

A bilingual who used Arabic and Somali with equal ease, Uways was a pamphleteer *par excellence*. According to oral tradition, he had composed dozens of pamphlets, ranging in subject from theology to Sufism.[19] He was also a poet of considerable powers (examples of his poetry will be cited shortly) and an innovator who was one of the first Somalis of learning to write Somali in Arabic script. A great many of his Somali poems were transmitted, disseminated, and preserved in this manner.[20] He was also a charismatic mystic who claimed an unrestricted access to the throne of Allah and to the fellowship of the saints. He "performed many miracles" and allowed, perhaps encouraged, his disciples to call him the "Master of the Time" (*Sahib al-Waqt*), and the title shows something of the millenarian strain in his teaching.

Uwaysiya Versus Saalihiya: Brotherhoods in Conflict

Although Sheikh Uways spent the greater part of his proselytizing activities in southern Somalia, he was apparently influential outside of Somalia, too. B. G. Martin shows, convincingly in my view, how the sheikh and his disciples fanned out from Zanzibar in numerous directions towards the East African interior as far as Tabora and Ujiji in the Great lakes region and the Yao country in what is today Malawi.[21] Yet to judge from subsequent events, Uways's was not the only movement popular with the Somalis at this time. While he was carrying the banner of revivalism in the south, a counter-movement was developing in the north, i.e., the Saalihiya. An off-shoot of Ahmadiya, the Saalihiya was to prove a lethal enemy of Uwaysiya. Saalihiya's parent order, the Ahmadiya, was already well established in Somalia, with several communal settlements in the Benaadir coast. In Merka, for example, the Ahmadiya challenged the influence of Sheikh Uways in the person of the Biyamaal chieftain, Sheikh 'Abdi Gafle, who effectively curbed the spread of the Uwaysiya among his kinsmen. But it was the Saalihiya, a neo-Sufist order, greatly influenced by Wahhabi doctrine, especially in its attack on the "cult of saints," that presented the greatest challenge to Sheikh Uways.[22]

The Saalihiya not only competed with Uwaysiya for the hearts of the Somalis, but it also questioned the doctrinal soundness of its rival, condemning many of Qaadiriya's ancient tenets as heretical. Saalihi adherents, for example, attacked as un-Islamic the Qaadiriya belief in the efficacy of the "intercessory powers of deceased saints" (*tawasul*). While believing with Qaadiriya in the transmission of blessing (*baraka*) by a living saint, Saalihis denied that a deceased saint has any *baraka* of validity to the living. In this way they condemned as erroneous the Qaadiriya practice of seeking intercession from their saints. Veneration of deceased saints, pilgrimages to their tombs, offering sacrifices on their behalf, ecstatic trances—practices Qaadiriya regularly engaged in—were viewed with horror by members of Saalihiya as polytheistic (shirk).

It was therefore not unlikely that a theological controversy should break out between members of the two orders. They traded vitriolic polemics in the first decade of the century which became exceptionally virulent towards 1908. On the Qaadiriya/Uwaysiya side, Uways himself led the attack. With a bitter pen dipped in injurious ink he inveighed against his rivals as "incestuous" apostates. The following, in B.G. Martin's competent translation, is an example:[23]

Blessed are Muhammad and his family
   Turn to them in every calamity
The person guided by Muhammad's law
   Will not follow the faction of Satan
Who deem it lawful to spill the blood of the learned
   Who take cash and women too: they are anarchists
They hinder the study of sciences
   Like law and grammar. They are the Karramiya*
To every dead Shaykh like al-Gilani
   They deny access to God, like the Janahiya**
Don't follow those men with big shocks of hair
   A coiffure like the Wahhabiya!
Publicly, they sell Paradise for cash
   In our land, they are a sect of dogs
Having permission, they dally with women
   Even their own mothers, which is nothing but incest
They follow their own subjective opinions

*The Karramiya, a Muslim sect of Iran, founded by Abu 'Abdallah Muhammad B. Karram (d. 225/869), shocked orthodox Muslims by suggesting that God had a body.
**The Janahiya adhered to the teachings of 'Abdullah b. Mu 'Awiya. Known also as the Tayyariya, this Shi'ite sect believed in reincarnation.

And no book of ours!
Their light is from the Devil
    They deny God at their dhikr
In word and action they are unbelievers
    Like their game of saying "God?"
"Lodge a complaint with Him!"
    How they are glorified by the Northerners
Great clamor they make, a moaning and groaning!
    A noise like the barking of curs
In divorce cases they augment the oaths
    But they abridge the religious ceremonies
They've gone astray and make others deviate on earth
    By land and sea amongst the Somalis
Have they no reason or understanding?
    Be not deceived by them
But flee as from a disaster
    From their infamy and unbelief.

That Sheikh Uways, the mild-mannered mystic who was nicknamed "Elegant-of-Tongue,"[24] was moved to fulminate against the Saalihiya in so violent a language does much to reveal the extent of bad blood between the two brotherhoods. By the phrase "they dally with women," Uways may have been making a not-so-oblique reference to Sayyid Muhammad's reputed weakness for sensuous pleasure. Uways, in any case, was not the only antagonist to charge the Sayyid with the moral foible of womanizing. The most memorable line, for example, of the poem "Call ye This Infidel a Mahdi?" ("*Ma Talyaanigaas Baa mahdi a?*")[25] by the poet 'Ali Jaama' Haabiil of the Habar Awal Isaaq, reads thus: "*Toddobuu gabaa naaga xor ah Tuu falaa daran e*" ("Of free women/he lecherously and routinely consorts with seven"). The point of the charge is that the Sayyid, in blatant contravention of the Qur'anic injunction that limits the number of wives a Muslim may have to four, routinely cohabited with seven consorts.

'Ali Duuh of the Dulbahante 'Ali Geri sublineage, and also another implacable poetic foe of the Sayyid, went even further and accused the Sayyid of incestuous conduct. In a viciously abusive epistle patently designed to injure the moral reputation of the Dervish leader, 'Ali Duuh sang joyously:[26]

Waa shaniyo toban naagahaad shurug wadaagtaan e
Sidii sumal shakaal looga furay ida shinkood jooga
Shabtaasuu ku hayn kama da'furo shiqibku naagaha e
Shaadır baa hablaha loogu waray shuul cus iyo cawr e
Inay Rooxa wada shaarugeen shookigay timid e

And the women you consort with are fifteen.
Like a fattened ram among sheep in heat,
He tires not of lust, the lecherous infidel;
In a crimson shawl and silken veil many an innocent lass night-visited
    him;
And lo, Rooho, his graceless sister, has come to the office testifying to
    partnership of lust!

Though even Dervish partisans would readily admit that the Sayyid had his share of the poet's flair for carnal pleasure, intemperate polemics by avowed enemies such as 'Ali Duuh, 'Ali jaama' or Sheikh Uways, for that matter, can hardly be taken as creditable guides to his personal morality. 'Ali Duuh, as the poet spokesman of the anti-Dervish faction of the 'Ali Geri, a lineage whose overwhelming majority supported the Dervishes, had strong motives for discrediting the Sayyid. The Sayyid, he thought, was leading 'Ali Duuh's kinsmen into a suicidal mission of folly and illusion. This proved to be a justifiable fear in the closing years of the Dervish struggle, when the 'Ali Geri were nearly wiped out from a combination of reprisal raids by British-protected clans and internal civil wars. The specter of 'Ali Geri calamities in fact inspired the Sayyid's most wrenching jeremiads in "The Scourge of Infidels" ("*Gaala-Leged*") poem, where he tearfully lamented:[27]

Cali Geri sidii loo gondoloy gobolba meel aadye
Waa gelengal nimankii fadhiyay guriga Ciideede
Eebbow gurbood baa hadhiyo gaban agoomeede

Alas, so grievously did oppression bear down upon the 'Ali Geri that
    they've been scattered into wandering fragments,
And the noble men of 'Id ('Ali Geri homesteads) have been utterly
    destroyed,
O God, only a cluster of hapless orphans have survived.

To return to the set of events touched off by Uways's ruinous attack on
the Dervishes, the Sayyid, who was a master at the craft of polemical exchange and who allegedly used to boast "Allah taught me the art of abuse
and acrimony," was never one to leave a poetic diatribe on him unanswered.
He responded to Qaadiriya charges with equal venom:[28]

Doodna waxaan u leeyahay kuwii diinta caasiyey
War hadii la kala diday sida deero iyo cawl
Rabbi nama dufeeye Cawar maxawla deristeen?
Eygi doofish lahaa daaha maxawgu rogateen?
Dumarkii idiin dhaxay dalaq maxawga yeesheen?
Doofaarkaad qalaysaan sow kama diqootaan?
Dulligiyo cadaabkii Maxaa kiin isugu daray?
Dariiqii rasuulkiyo dwagii maxawga bayrteen?

A word to the backsliding apostates:
When the holy separated from the wicked,
    as deer from gazelle*

---

*Somalis believe that the gazelles and deer never mix although ecological scarcity
may force them to graze in the same pasturefields. Similarly, the poet's argument
runs, the godly and the wicked do not mix even if the necessities of life force them

God pardon us! How is it that you
 absconded with Bad-Eye*
Forsaking your lawful wives,
 how have you opted to cohabit with the hairy dog**
And it never fills you with revulsion that you should
 continue to skin the pigs,
In addition to degradation, how is it
 that you earned hell?
What on earth! since when did you turn
 a progeny of the Evil One?
Why have you gone astray
 from the Prophet's way, the Straight Path?
Why is the Truth, so plain
 so hidden from you?

In time, the verbal assaults began to turn into physical attacks. To judge from local accounts, Uways had what might be termed in modern jargon a "martyr complex." In his repeated forays into Saalihiya theology and territory, he might have been courting death, and his chronicler records frequently the sheikh's wish to die a martyr's death.[29] A man of action as well as words, Uways was apparently not satisfied with mere polemics. As Saalihiya was sweeping the north, already having converted the Dulbahante and Warsangali Daarood, the majority of the Habar Tol Ja'alo Isaaq in the north and the central sections of the Ogaadeen Daarood, Uways made the fateful decision to move northwards in 1909, possibly to counter the advancing Saalihiya

to be neighbors.

 *Col. H. E. Swayne, commander of British operations against the Dervishes was badly wounded in the left eye at the battle of Eeragoy (1901), and so came to be nicknamed Bad-Eye ('Awar).

 **Hairy Dog was also Col. Swayne, whom the sun-smoothed Somalis found remarkably hirsute.

influence in the Shabeele valley. His party suddenly came upon a force of Jidle tribesmen who were doctrinally inclined to the Saalihiya teaching. The Jidle were out to punish the Rahanwayn, their bitter enemies and followers of Uways, who had severely raided them the previous month. Thus, they had no reason to view the sheikh with favor. They attacked his settlement at Biyooley, some 300 kms inland, on 14 April 1909, murdering the sheikh and all but one of his twenty-seven disciples. The survivor was Abdulqaadir Maanazayli who was later to compose a moving ode (*qasiida*) describing the raid. Entitled "*Uways Ahmad Waliya Allah*," [30] this piece contains material of historical significance and is now incorporated into the liturgy of the Uwaysiya order. In one passage, for instance, the author observes:[31]

> They came in the blazing sun of the morning,
> Some on horseback, some on foot,
> Crying "Muhammad Salih is our succor, Muhammad Salih is our
>   refuge."
> But Uways—the saint of God—resplendent, calm, serene,
> Replied, "Majesty is the Lord's, Great is our God."
> They snuffed out his precious life.
> Oh, Sheikh Uways, the Saint,
> How majestic, how heroic, he bore the sting of death!
> Oh, the oppressors of mankind prosper not,
> Oh, how much less would it be with the oppressors of the Lord's
>   anointed!

Uways's religious prestige was such that even his enemies seem to have acknowledged it grudgingly. His murderers are said to have "truly repented of their deed"[32] and offered special sacrifices as acts of penance. But the pang of conscience was apparently not shared by Sayyid Muhammad. Upon learning of Uways's death, he dashed off a valedictory victory hymn, celebrating with an almost obscene mirth the news of the sheikh's fall. He sang:[33]

Candhadogoble Goortaan dilaa
   Roobki noo da'aye

Behold, at long last,
When we slew the old wizard,
The rains began to come!

Legacy of Bitterness

Sayyid Muhammad's poetic diatribe, gloating over the fall of his distinguished rival, provides a clue to his deep antipathy toward Sheikh Uways. While overt hostilities between the two movements have ceased in recent years, the sentiment of mutual distrust and hate continues to poison their relations. Nowhere is this more evident than in the emotional fervor with which members of Uwaysiya commemorate the martyrdom of their spiritual leaders. In regular Uwaysiya *dhikrs* (ecstatic dance), the high mark of congregational worship occurs with the chanting of ardent panegyrics dedicated to the memory of the martyred saint. These eulogies evoke passionately the virtues and merits of the sheikh; they also serve as a constant reminder that his life had been "snuffed out" by members of a "satanic faction," the Saalihiya.

In addition to these *dhikrs*, the Uwaysiya observe an annual pilgrimage (*siyaaro*) to the sheikh's tomb—around which a cult of veneration has grown—in the Islamic month of Rabi' al-Awal. During this period members of the faithful come from as far as Tanzania to hold a week of spiritual revival in which believers engage in communal meditation and heart-searching repentance. It is a period of intense religious ecstasy: large numbers of animals are sacrificed; charity is given to the poor; blessings are sought and obtained, and forgiveness of sin collectively prayed for. This week ends with a huge *dhikr* circle that usually begins around 5 P.M. and lasts late into the night. Intensely emotional, this *dhikr* seems to have the elements of a passion play, with the protracted chanting, dancing, and rhythmic body movement producing a form of collective, spiritual delirium, causing some individuals to experience an involuntary convulsion.

The praise odes sung in his honor evoke vividly the manner of the sheikh's death. Significantly, they also elevate his virtues almost to the level of those of the Prophet, as this refrain of a commonly sung eulogy illustrates:[34]

Alla la ilaha Illalah
Muhammad Rasul Allah
Sheikh 'Abdulqaadir shaylilah
Uways Ahmad waliya Allah

Hallelujah! There is no god but God
Muhammad is His apostle
The Blessed 'Abdulqaadir is our succor
And Uways Ahmad is Allah's friend

Sheikh Uways and Sayyid Muhammad in Comparative Perspective

For purposes of conceptual grasp and analytical clarity, it may be helpful to conclude this discussion with a brief assessment of the roles played respectively by the Sayyid and the sheikh in Somali history. Mention was made at the beginning of this article of the great public tribute in print and official pronouncements paid to the Sayyid and his resistance movement over the last twenty years for their contribution to the growth of Somali national identity. For the most part this has been deserved praise. By contrast, Sheikh Uways and his reformist movement attracted precious little attention from either the Somali academic community or government leaders. They have been neglected by all except the humble folk who revere the memory of their master in meekness and unobtrusive quiescence. Has this been a deserved silence? If a case can be made—as I will attempt to do shortly—that the position of Sheikh Uways in Somali history is no less eminent than that of the Sayyid, what explains the official silence? Clannish or regional considerations?

To deal adequately with the respective places of the Sayyid and the sheikh in Somali history, it is necessary to explore briefly what the fundamental cornerstones of the Somali national experience consist of. On this question we should turn for help to the late president of the Somali Republic, Dr. 'Abdirashiid 'Ali Shermaarke, who laid down what he regarded as the core of moral and ethical principles that informs the somali national consciousness and accounts for its startling uniqueness in eastern Africa. According to Shermaarke, the Somali nation rests on two central pillars "of inestimable value: the teaching of Islam on the one hand and lyric poetry on the other."[35] Islamic precepts and oral poetry, he argued, constitute the essence of Somalism, explaining the peculiar cultural cohesiveness and political resilience that save the Somalis from disintegrating under the trials of repeated setbacks, both domestically and externally.

Shermaarke's observation is a stroke of enlightenment. In Islam a Somali imbibes the spiritual and moral fortitude necessary to embrace the challenges of life, to face adversity with a measure of calm equanimity that would astonish Westerners. "*Insha All, khayr bay ahaan*" ("God willing, it will be well with us") is a favorite motto, often on the lips of Somalis. It is a motto to conjure with; it helps one get through the day; it insists on an attitude of optimism in the face of hardship; it affirms life. And it serves to evoke the mixture of hope, serenity, and hardheaded determination to survive, which the spirit of al-Islam has helped inculcate in Somali consciousness over the years.

Oral poetry, on the other hand, fosters in the Somalis a climate of national solidarity by molding the varied, and sometimes discordant, ethnic and regional segments of Somali society into a unified cultural community with a common language, common myths, common aesthetic values as well as a shared outlook toward life. It binds together nomad and city dweller, peasant and fisherman, and rich and poor into a collective intellectual psyche. Oral poetry for the Somalis has the force of ritual, serving, in Sheikh Jaama"s informed judgement, as "the central integrating principle without which harmonious relations in life would be unthinkable."[36] To put the elder's observation in a different perspective, it is through the medium of oral poetry that Somalis ask the abiding questions: Whence come we? What are we? Whither go we?

The vitality of the twin heritage of faith and verse for Somali life casts into a sharp perspective the nature of the individual achievements of the Sayyid and the sheikh. As the greatest Somali poet of the twentieth century, perhaps the greatest ever in the Somali language, the Sayyid was (and is) the literary mind of the Somalis. Sheikh Uways, the quiet mystic, who is alleged to have radiated the "irresistible, cosmic light of the divine,"[37] was (and is), in a manner of speaking, the heart of the Somalis.

At the risk of digressing from the central point, I am tempted to advance here some heretical views, which may well ruffle the historical convictions of those who strongly adhere to conventional interpretations of the Somali past. The Sayyid, I submit, has been vastly overrated on several fronts, and the time has come to inject into his assessment some salutary revisionism.

First, there is the question of the significance of his religious contribution. Was the Sayyid the inspiration for a great spiritual revival on the order, say, of Sheikh Uways's? Did his Saalihiya movement reinvigorate Somali spiritual life and reawaken the Muslims of eastern Africa, as manifestly the Uwaysiya did? The confinement of space here does not permit an extended exploration of this problem. On balance, however, intellectual honesty should incline an objective, informed observer to respond negatively to the above questions.

To be sure, the Saalihiya brotherhood produced in the years between 1987 and 1910 a considerable burst of energy, creating a renewed sense of spiritual fervor and moral regeneration in the hearts of many Somalis. But this had been largely a negative energy. As new, militant converts, many Saalihis tended to be self-righteous, disagreeably smug, and, on occasion, to behave in a manner that bordered on spiritual bigotry. This is perhaps a characteristic condition of all new converts. In order to contest Qaadiriya's grip on the hearts and minds of the Somalis, they impugned with unbrotherly zeal the venerable beliefs of the latter order. In doing so, they threatened to engulf the Somalis in a fratricidal war. That Sheikh Uways's murder by Saalihiya adherents did not provoke disastrous reprisals from his followers must have been a fortunate development. Perhaps the fact that the sheikh's devotees were largely southern peasant farmers of pacific disposition, unlike the warlike nomadic partisans of Saalihiya, spared Somalia from genocidal warfare.

A second problematic area is that of the Sayyid's contribution to Somali nationalism. That the roving holy man and his ragtag army managed to hold off for over twenty years the combined forces of three colonial powers, including the mightiest European power, surely constitutes a heroic event, rarely paralleled in the annals of African resistance to European imperialism. Though the Sayyid failed in his stated objective of driving out imperialists, black and white, from the Somali peninsula and though at the end of his valiant efforts the colonial grip on the Somalis was more firm than ever, his failure compels in the Somalis a deserved admiration for a hero whose failure is at once tragic and ennobling. But on the other side of the scale, the struggle's cost, in life and property to the Somalis, was unjustifiably high.

By a conservative estimate, some 200,000 Somalis—a hefty one-third of the population of northern Somalia—lost their lives as a result of the anti-colonial struggle, not to mention the widespread destruction of property and the attendant social dislocation and economic ruin. As the poet Shire Idaad put it, the Dervish war of resistance and colonial campaigns to suppress it proved to be a "universal perdition" from which "not a path hath escaped unscathed."[38] Was the effort worth the price? Moreover, if the Sayyid had succeeded in driving the colonialists out and established himself in power, would he have imposed on Somalia an autocratic theocracy based on doctrinaire interpretation of esoteric Saalihiya liturgy? And if this had happened, would not the Somali majority who espoused Qaadiriya belief have resisted his rule? And if they had done so, given the Sayyid's demonstrated habit of giving no quarter to those who resisted his authority, would the outcome of such a resistance have been an organized, internecine bloodletting? These are difficult questions which defy easy answers. But they do serve to inspire some thoughts towards a healthy demythologizing of the man and his movement.

The final point to consider (which is in essence a corollary of the above) concerns the Sayyid's intellectual contribution to Somali religious thought. Obviously, he was a theologian of considerable depth and erudition, though to my mind, not of the same class as "heavy weights" such as Sheikh Uways and his disciple, 'Abdullaahi Qutbi. Intellectually, the Sayyid belonged to the broad movement of late nineteenth century African Islam that B.G. Martin described as "neo-Sufists."[39] Influenced by Muhammad 'Abd al-Wahhab's (1115–1201/1703–1787) literalist interpretation of the Qur'an and Hadith, neo-Sufists favored a literal, strict reading of the holy books. Suspicious of such juristic methods as *qiyas* (analogy) and *ijma'* (judicial consensus) adopted by classical Muslim judges, the neo-Sufists tended to apply scriptural injunctions literally to social problems. The Sayyid, for example, did not recoil from amputating the hands and feet of convicted thieves nor from public flogging of adulterers, as laid down by Qur'anic precepts.

The most extended exposition of the Sayyid's mind as a Muslim thinker occurs in *Risala Lil Biyamaal* (Letter to the Biyamaal Clan), preserved for many years in manuscript form by the diligent care of Sheik Muhammad A. Liibaan of the Somali Academy. It was published as part of *Somaliya: Antologia Storico-Culturale* (in 1967).[40]

Numerically powerful, traditionally fierce warriors and religiously inclined towards Ahmadiya, the Biyamaal possessed resources which must have intrigued the Poor Man of God, a humble title the Sayyid, like other Sufis of his time, was fond of sporting. More than this, the Biyamaal mounted a major resistance effort against the Italians in the first decade of the nineteenth century, a response that induced the Italians to carry out a series of brutal punitive expeditions against them. They were repeatedly harried by overzealous Italian pacification campaigns. As a result, the Biyamaal had good reason to be interested in joining the Dervish cause. The Sayyid, for his part, had a natural incentive to win the support of this powerful clan who dominated the approaches to the strategic Benaadir port of Merka. This explains why he had taken the time to put forward to them a detailed theological statement concerning his reasons for leading a resistance war.

The central point of the *Letter* concerns the Sayyid's attempt to make the doctrinal and theological case for waging a *jihad* not only against the "infidels" but also against Somali Muslims who refused to join his cause. Though his argument bristles with the rigid literalism of Muhammad 'Abdul-

Wahhab, the Sayyid on occasion shows brilliant flashes of creative imagination. Consider, for instance, this passage from which he develops an argument for the *jihad* from the example of the dedication and humility of
Christian monks:[41]

* * * * ARABIC INSERT HERE * * * *

As for the holy war [*jihad*], it is a religious duty. The Apostle—may
peace be upon him—said: I charge you to fear God because this is the
foundation of all worship. Also, the holy struggle is a religious
obligation because the *jihad* is the monastic institution of Islam. That
is, for Christians the monastic life is the most meritorious form of
worship. In Islam, by contrast, no deed is more worthy than *jihad*. The
monastic institution in fact stems from avoidance based on fear. The
Christians used to cloister themselves up in order to avoid worldly
cares, to abandon worldly enjoyment and to shun worldly people, and
to bear humbly the burdens of this world, to the extent that one could
find among them an individual who would castrate himself and place
a chain around his neck and do other self-torturing things.

The Prophet forbade such deeds in Islam. He enjoined Muslims
from subjecting themselves to such bodily harm. Instead he ordered
them to do *jihad*, . . . because for Muslims there is no devotional act
more meritorious than to degrade oneself in the service [*jihad*] of
God. . . .

It must have taken a lively imagination to transform the quiet piety of
Christian hermits into a doctrine for a holy war! What about the Sayyid as
an Arabic prose-writer? If we leave aside his published writings (which are
likely to have been tampered with by over-zealous editors) and look at his
unpublished material as standards by which to judge his essayistic capacities,
what we find is most disconcerting. Here is a random sample from one of his
letters preserved in British archives:[42]

* * * * ARABIC INSERT HERE * * * *

Praise be to God in every circumstance. After: this letter comes from Mahammad 'Abdullah Hasan and the rest of the Dervishes to General Swayne. The purpose of the letter is, first, to inform you that our delegation returned to us and they have informed me that you have treated them with courtesy and that you have settled the disturbances in the land. They also informed us that you said you would leave the country, I mean the country of the Nugaal and Buuhoodle and its neighborhoods. This news made us extremely joyous. They further informed us of your wish that there should be no more war in the land in our lifetime. They also informed us that you are well disposed towards us. Let it be known to you that as of now we have accepted the peace treaty and that there will be no trouble from us. Should we receive trouble from your people, we will let you know. We will not move against them without first notifying you of our intended action. We also wish to inform you that the country is at peace; no one should be afraid of us; if a person or persons come to us, we will treat them well. This is one thing.[*]

Was the Sayyid's level of Arabic proficiency so primitive as to produce this syntactic gobbledygook? The most charitable thing is to assume that the letter was authored not by him but by one of his barely literate scribes and that he neglected to peruse first what he was about to put his name to. There are however two problems with this assumption. First, the handwriting of the letter bears striking resemblance to the Sayyid's handwriting elsewhere. If a scribe had written it, he must have possessed an extraordinary talent for hand imitation. Second, the quality of the Arabic in the entire collection scarcely does better than the produced sample. Stylistically, the language in nearly all the letters is rather shoddy, riddled as it is with shabby Yemeni colloquialisms of the market sort. Were these letters written by the Sayyid?

---

[*]This is an edited rendition. A literal translation would be difficult to follow.

A careful scrutiny would lead a reasonable student to conclude that they were. What, however, do Arabic deficiencies matter in the literacy genius who produced such Somali masterpieces as "The Scourge of Infidels" ("*Gaala-Legend*"), "The Double-Dealer" ("*Musuqmaasuq*"), "A Hymn of Thanksgiving" ("*Mahade Haw Sheego*"), "The Herald of Good Tidings" ("*Bishaarooyinkii Eebahay*"), and "The Will" ("*Dardaaran*").

These poems and others of equal brilliance and insight, which cannot be named here, constitute the priceless treasure the Sayyid had left the Somalis. No Somali with adequate command of the language and a modest literary inclination who has had the Sayyid's poems chanted or recited to him will think the same about the world again, if he thinks at all. Through the power of his tongue the Sayyid did much to shape the collective mind of the Somali national consciousness in the same way, perhaps, that the Ukrainian nationalist poet Taras Shevchenko is credited with the creation of a Ukrainian national identity, to the lasting consternation of the Russians.[43]

Uways, in contrast to the Sayyid, had a masterful command of Arabic but was an unmitigated disaster in Somali. While his Arabic compositions sparkle with energy and style, as the poem cited earlier attests, his Somali compositions represent a disconcerting example of linguistic horrors. A caveat must be noted here: The sheikh's Somali material is in the Rahanwayn dialect, which, though I understand haltingly, I do not speak. Thus it may well be that others more adept at it will find greater literary merits than I did. It is also the case though that, while doing field work in 1977, I showed some of this material in April of that year to some Rahanwayn elders in the town of Hudur with the idea of soliciting their opinion on the literary values of Sheikh Uways's Somali material, and I found them nearly as unimpressed by it as I had been. They seemed to have revered Sheikh Uways the mystic, not the doggerel writer.)

Even in Arabic (of which, as I said earlier, the Sheikh had a masterly grasp), he ran into trouble when he was in a deep spiritual ecstasy (*jithba*)—which was often. At such times the sheikh simply could not keep his mysticism from interfering with his writing. His student and hagiographer admits as much:[44]

* * * * ARABIC INSERT HERE * * * *

He (Uways) was at times in a spiritual trance, especially in matters of prose and poetic composition. For this reason, many of his versifications do not conform to established metrical and syntactic rules. This did not bother the sheikh, because he was an experienced hand at the fundamental elements of composition. Once one of the Sheikhs told me that he joined Uways while he was giving some hortatory thoughts to the people. In his talk he said: There are sixteen principles (lit. seas of grammar) of composition whose uses are well-known among people. Then he said: Among them are some archaic ones, and these predominate in my poetry as, for example, in the devotional hymn "Majesty Is the Lord's."

A useful example of the Sheikh's literary offenses when under the influence of *jithba* is his praise ode "*Ayaa Sa'ii Ilal Maula.*"[45] Every one of its fifty odd lines ends in "*Allahu,*" an agreeable sentiment for a worshipful heart but an unrewarding platitude to a thinking mind. Repetitive trivia and flat utterances come in such a higgledy-piggledy frequency as to induce a sober reader to yawn and put it away quickly. It reads as though the demands of syntax became an irrelevant nuisance to the sheikh in the face of the ecstatic strivings of the heart to become "the friend of God" ("*Waliya Allah*").

In summary, Sheikh Uways not only powerfully revitalized Somali Islam, but also made the Benaadir coast the Mecca of eastern Africa, attracting pilgrims and disciples from far and wide, from as far as what is today eastern Zaire to Malawi and from Tanzania to Uganda, and the lands in between. The needy, the hungry, and the seeking (*muriids*) came to him to receive spiritual and physical nourishment. His presence calmed jarred nerves. The Sayyid's, on the other hand, caused creative hysteria. To take a distant but not irrelevant analogy, the Sayyid was the Shakespeare of the Somalis, Sheikh Uways their Martin Luther. This is no small praise for either man.

Notes

1. For a general treatment of the Qaadiriya and its role in Somali religious life, see I. M. Lewis, *A Pastoral Democracy*. London: Oxford University Press, 1961, Chapter 7; for the influence of Qaadiriya in southern Somalia, see Lee V. Cassanelli, "The Benaadir past: Essays in southern Somali History," Ph.D. dissertation, University of Wisconsin, 1973, pp. 43–69; for a brief but perceptive discussion of Uwaysiya in southern Somalia and East Africa, see B. G. Martin, *Muslim Brotherhoods in Nineteenth-Century Africa.* Cambridge: Cambridge Universi ty Press, 1976, pp. 158–176.

2. The statement is based on Sheikh 'Ali Sa'iid's estimate of the number of northern Somali Hajj-makers in the 1890s, as opposed to those in the 1910s. Sheikh 'Ali is the head of the Saalihiya order in Bur'o and he has a reputation for knowledge on the history of Muslim orders in Somalia. His estimate that ten percent of the male population of Berbera made the *hajj* can be regarded as a well-informed guess. He attributes the high proportion of *hajj* makers in the 1890s to an unusual prosperity of the clans during this time, which enabled many to afford the cost of pilgrimage.

3. For African Islam, this theme receives a brief but provocative treatment in B. G. Martin, *Muslim Brotherhoods.*

4. R. Coupland, *East Africa and Its Invaders*. New York: Russell 7 Russell. 2nd ed. 1965, pp. 453–4.

5. E. Hertslet, *The Map of Africa By Treaty.* London: Frank Cass & Co., 3rd ed., 1967, pp. 304–308.

6. A phrase coined by Czar Alexander I.

7. Ronald Robinson and John Gallagher, *Africa and the Victorians.* London: MacMillan Press, 1961, pp. 79–81.

8. The Qur'an, Sura III:110.

9. For the special significance of history to the Muslim *ummah* as the embodiment of divine experiment on earth, see Wilfred C. Smith. *Islam in Modern History,* Princeton, New Jersey: Princeton University Press, 1957, pp. 3–40.

10. J. S. Trimingham, *Sufi Orders in Islam.* Oxford: Clarendon Press, 1971.

11. Martin, *Muslim Brotherhoods.*

12. To be sure, belief in the millenarian, the notion of the coming Mahdi or prince-judge under whose government holiness, righteousness and justice will be triumphant as sin, wickedness, and oppression banished from the earth, is an undercurrent theme in Muslim eschatology and the *Mahdist* figure frequently appears in the history of Muslim societies. See the *Encyclopedia of Islam*. M. Th. Houtsma and A. J. Wendink (eds.) Vol. II, 1936, pp. 11–114.
13. Martin, *Muslim Brotherhoods*, pp. 5–6.
14. *The Qur'an*, Sura I:5.
15. 'Abdirahman 'Umar al-Qadirii, *Jala' al-'Aynayn*, Cairo, N.D. (ca. 1954) and Cairo, 1383 h=1964.
16. Uways's grandson, Uways Muhiyadiin Uways, bases his claim to the spiritual leadership of the East Africa Qaadiriya to his grandfather's ordination by Salman.
17. al-Qadiri, *Jala al-'Alnayn*, pp. 3–10; cf. *Jawhar*, pp. 9–10.
18. This note and those following come from fieldnotes compiled during my field research (January—July 1977) in Kenya and Somalia as part of the work for a doctoral dissertation at Northwestern University. The project was jointly funded by a grant from the Social Science Research Council and Northwestern's Graduate School. Here is the method I follow in quoting from the notes: I first identify the source by the word "fieldnotes," then place and date of interview and where applicable the page number of the fieldnotes. Thus in the present example: Sheikh Abukar Mahammad Yare, general manager of Uwaysiya's spiritual and material affairs, "Fieldnotes," Biyooley, Somalia, April 13, 1977.
19. Two of these pamphlets are in the possession of Abukar Mahammad Yare, see preceding note.
20. "*Nabtha min ba'd al-Tarikh Sheikh Uways,*" an authorless manuscript in the possession of Uways's grandson and present spiritual leader of the Uwaysiya brotherhood.
21. Martin, *Muslim Brotherhoods*, pp. 164–165.
22. Wahhabism was founded by Muhammad 'Abdul-Wahhab (1115–1201/1703–1787). The teachings of this puritanical movement, especially as promulgated by its great apologist, Ibn Tayyini, rejected the intercessory powers of saints, maintaining that it was *shirk* (polytheistic) to seek intercession from a dead saint. See *Encyclopedia of Islam*, p. 1086. Although politically the Wahhabi doctrines

were on the rise in Somalia, they did not claim many adherents.

23. Quoted in Martin, *Muslim Brotherhoods,* pp. 161–162.

24. Al-Qadir, *Jawhar,* p. 15.

25. Aw Daahir Afqarshe. "Fieldnotes." Mogadishu, February 25, 1977, p. 12.

26. Sheikh Jaama' 'Umaar 'Iise, "Fieldnotes." Mogaidhsu, February 18, 1977, p. 194.

27. Sheikh Jaama' (Aw Jaamac Cumar Ciise), *Diiwaanka Gabayadii Sayid Maxamad Cabdulle Xasan. Ururintii Koowaad.,* Mogadishu (Xamar): Wasaaradda Hiddaha iyo Tacliintaa Sare, 1974. p. 230.

28. Sheikh Jaama' (Aw Jaamac), *Diiwaanku,* p. 100.

29. "Nabtha min ba' d al-Tarikh Sheikh Uways," see note 20.

30. Uways's father was called Mahammad, but the Somalis use the names Muhammad and Ahmad interchangeably.

31. Excerpt from tape-recording of "Uways Ahmad Waliya Allah," recorded April 13, 1977 at Biyooley.

32. Haajiya Sittah, Uways's daughter, claimed that one of the leaders, Nuur Jira', of the attacking party returned to the burning camp, shaken at learning that the victim was none other than the Uways. He expiated the "wicked deeds" of his comrades by providing a safe conduct to the wives and children of the massacred Qaadiriya. "Fieldnotes," Biyooley, april 14–16, 1977.

33. From the Sayyid's poem *"Candhadogoble."* A point of interest may be the varying significance that the two groups seem to attach to the rain, floods, and hurricane allegedly attendant on the sheikh's death. To the followers of the sheikh, it represented a disruption of the natural order and a manifestation of the divine displeasure that befell the Dervishes and caused them heavy losses by blocking their retreat routes and complicating their logistics and get-away. To the Dervishes, on the other hand, the death of a heretic constituted a divine favor bringing rain and other blessings.

34. See note 31.

35. Quoted in Somali Government. *The Somali Peninsula: New Light on Imperial Motives.* London: Stapler Printers, 1963, p. V.

36. Cited in Said S. Samatar, *Oral Poetry and Somali Nationalism: The Case of Sayyid Mahammad 'Abdille Hasan.*

37. Sheikh Abukar Mahammad Yare, "Fieldnotes," see note 17.

38. Cited in Samatar, *Oral Poetry*, p. 161; also see Aw Daahir Afqarshe. "Fieldnotes," p. 12.
39. Martin, *Muslim Brotherhoods,*, pp. 1–9.
40. *Somaliya: Antologia Storico-Culturale, No. 3.* Mogadishu: Ministero Publica Istruzione, 1967.
41. *Ibid.,* pp. 8–9.
42. Source: C.O. 535/1, enclosed in Dispatch 01876, Public Records office, London.
43. For understanding the importance of this poet to Ukrainian nationalism, I am indebted to Professor Taras Hunczak, a noted Ukrainian scholar at Rutgers University, Fall 1984.
44. Sheikh 'Abdul-Rahman, *Jawhar,* p. 12.
45. *Ibid.,* pp. 66–72.

CHAPTER FOUR

Islam as a Resistance Ideology among the Oromo of Ethiopia

The Wallo Case, 1700–1900

MOHAMMED HASSEN

BEFORE EMBARKING ON THE MAIN subject, I would like to make a few pertinent remarks about the Oromo people, who until recently were known as Galla, a term loaded with negative connotations. The Oromo do not call themselves Galla and they resist being called so. In this chapter, I employ Oromo, the name that they have always used.

The Oromo, who constitute a good half of the population of Ethiopia, are the single largest national group in the Horn of Africa. They are also one of the major African peoples. The Oromo belong to the Eastern Cushitic-language speaking group of peoples who are known to have lived in the Ethiopian region for thousands of years. In fact, it is said that more than half of the speakers of the Cushitic languages are Oromo or speak Afaan Oromo, the Oromo language[1] that is also the third largest Afro-Asiatic language in the world after Arabic and Hausa.[2] We do not know when the Oromo evolved their separate national identity and language, but we do know that they are one of the indigenous peoples of Ethiopia[3] who had lived in the highlands of southern Ethiopia for the greatest part of their history. In fact, the Muslim state of Bali, the Northern part of the present administrative region of Bale[4] is believed to have been the original home of the primeval Oromo group, which practiced barley cultivation.[5] The implication of the connection between the Muslim state of historical Bali and early Oromo history will become clear further on in this discussion. Here it should suffice to say:

> . . . Professor Haberland believes, and rightly, that the ancestral home of the Oromo was in the cool highlands in the region of Bale. In one Oromo tradition, there is a reference to a faraway land, the land which is consistently claimed as the first home of the Oromo people, the birth of the nation. This land is known as Fugug. . . . Today, the land of Fugug and Mount Fugug are located in the administrative region of Arsi, the heartland of historical Bali. The Oromo people who lived in the highlands of Bali engaged in mixed farming, while the lowlands in the valley of river Ganale became the grazing ground for the pastoralists who drifted away from the main group due to the transhumant nature of their economy.[6]

About seventy percent of the Oromo are Muslims. This means the Oromo are the single largest Muslim national group in the Horn of Africa. Islam spread among the Oromo much later than among the Somalis, the second major Muslim national group in the Horn of Africa. A great deal has been written on the role of Islam among the Somali, while very little, if any, has been written about Islam among the Oromo. Thus far, no article has been published on Islam as an ideology of resistance for Muslim Oromo. Until recently the common theme that runs through the extremely meager literature on the subject is the perception and the assumption that Islam spread among the Oromo quite recently[7] and that it did not influence their traditional institutions before their conversion during the nineteenth century. The significance of Islam as a possible factor shaping at least two aspects of

Oromo institutions, as early as the fourteenth century, has never been mentioned, much less discussed. The humble aim of this chapter is not to describe the process of the spread of Islam among the Oromo (which may be a topic for a book) but to fulfill two interrelated objectives.

The first objective is to establish Islamic influence on some aspects of Oromo institutions dating back to the fourteenth century. This is a fascinating thesis as well as a controversial subject. Fascinating because the thesis is new and its implications could have far-reaching consequences for the history of the Oromo and that of Islam in Ethiopia. Controversial because the thesis is a radical departure from the established historical wisdom that limits the spread of Islam among the Oromo to the nineteenth century and after. The evidence in support of the thesis is not new. It is, however, a new interpretation of existing data even though that interpretation does not have the support of scholarly works hitherto undertaken. I believe further research in the future will substantiate and confirm that Islam influenced some aspects of the Oromo institutions much earlier than hitherto assumed.

The second objective, of this chapter, is an attempt to demonstrate that Islam played a crucial role not only as a source of Oromo cultural identity, but more importantly as an ideology of resistance against Christian territorial expansion, political domination, religious persecution, and economic exploitation. Trimingham's argument that "the shock of the ruthless military conquests of the Abyssinians which broke up much of their tribal constitution and customary sanctions opened the way to Islamic infiltration"[8] among the oromo could be correct only if this argument means that Islam spread rapidly among the Arsi and Harar Oromo after they were conquered by King Menilek of Shawa in the 1880s. In Wallo, where the Oromo embraced Islam during the seventeenth century, the pressure from the neighboring Christian polity turned Islam into an ideology of resistance capable of mobilizing human and material resources, and it became the battle cry for the struggle. In the process Islam succeeded in solidly establishing itself among the Oromo and remained an important part of their cultural life.

This chapter is divided into two parts: The first part deals with Islamic influence on two Oromo institutions. This is necessary in order to establish the long connection the Oromo people had with Islam. The second part deals with Islam as an ideology of resistance from about 1700 to 1889.

Islamic Influence on Two Oromo Institutions

Though Islam had reached the Red Sea Coast of the Horn of Africa during the life-time of its founder/prophet Muhammad, it did not gain any political influence before the beginning of the tenth century. As elsewhere in Africa, trade played a very crucial role in the spread and consolidation of Islam in Ethiopia, where initially traders, were the teachers, preachers, and the ideological arm of Islam. The Islamic current brought by merchants and traders cum preachers powerfully affected the formation of states between the port of Zeyla and the rich highlands of southern Ethiopia. Thus between the tenth and thirteenth centuries, a number of Muslim states, such as Shawa, Ifat, Dawaro, Fatagar, Hadiya, Waj, Adal, and Bali came into existence.

Islam gave the rulers of these states a means of governing bigger and more complex political structures by providing them ideological unity as well as access to the current of Islamic thought which enabled them to transcend the narrow parochial loyalty. Islam also provided a sort of international passport for traders, teachers and preachers, to dwell in and move freely between these states. The above mentioned Muslim states were conquered one after the other by Emperor Amda-Siyon (1314–1344), the founder of the Medieval Christian Empire of Abyssinia. Of all the Muslim states conquered by Amda-Siyon (between 1329 and 1332[9]), Bali seems to have influenced the early history of the Oromo nation.

This history of the Muslim state of Bali is intimately linked with the history of Sheikh Hussein, the great thirteenth century standard bearer of Islam in Bali. Sheikh Hussein was a Muslim scholar of Arab Origin. He remains the single most accomplished missionary saint in southern Ethiopia. The life story of this missionary, the ultimate paradigm of saintly virtues and powers (baraka) is an integral part of the history of Bali, which was also the original home of the primeval Oromo group that practiced barley cultivation. The Oromo calendar and the Qallu institution seem to have developed at the time the Oromo lived in historical Bali, as both show unmistakable Islamic influence.

The Oromo Calendar

The calendar, which was the foundation of the Gada System (participatory form of traditional Oromo democracy), seems to have developed before the separation of the Oromo and their sixteenth-century migration. This is because the core of the calendar is more or less the same everywhere,[10] notwithstanding the absence of physical contact for the past four to five hundred years among the people who spread over a wide territory. The Oromo calendar is:

> a permutation calendar the like of which has been recorded only three times in the history of mankind. It occurs among the Chinese, the Hindu and the Mayans—three civilizations far removed from [the Oromo].[11]

Two noted scholars have different versions of the origin of the Oromo calendar. On the one hand, Haberland believes that the foreign origin of the Oromo calendar is unquestionable.[12] However, the good professor failed to show us where the foreign origin came from. On the other hand, Professor Asmarom Legesse thinks the calendar is one of the highest achievements of the Oromo.[13] Neither of them suspects Islamic influence on this calendar, which was a combination of Islamic influence and the indigenous Oromo (Cushitic) element. In fact, there has been obvious influence from Muslim (Arabic and Persian) and Christian (Amhara) calendars.[14] The crucial question is: Where did the influence from the three foreign calendars meet with the Oromo Cushitic element, cross-fertilizing with it to produce one of the most sophisticated and highly developed[15] oral calendars in the world? Some of the trading Muslim states of southern Ethiopia would be the likely areas for the conception of this calendar.

However, it seems to me that the Muslim state of Bali, the original home of the primeval Oromo group, with the shrine of Sheikh Hussein as the rallying point for all the Muslims of Southern Ethiopia was the most likely place. Historical Bali, with its weaving industry, its foreign traders, its relatively large Arab community including some Persians, as well as Christian administrators and military colonists, could be the most likely place where the Oromo calendar took its shape under different pressures. It is impossible to say in which period this occurred. It may have happened between the fourteenth and fifteenth centuries, since by the end of the fifteenth century, the Gada System, which was inextricably linked with the calendar and operated on accurate measurement of time, was already a full-fledged military, political, economic, social, and ritual institution of the Oromo society. In short, Islamic influence on the Oromo calendar is unquestionable. Such an influence is even more pronounced on the Oromo institution, discussed below.

The Qallu Institution

A Qallu was a high priest, who was the spiritual leader of Oromo traditional religion. The term Qallu stands for the institution and for the high priest, who guarded the law of Waqa and its interpretation. Waqa was the tradition-al Oromo (Cushitic) God, the creator of the universe, and the sustainer of life on earth. When reduced to the essential, both the Qallu institution and its relation with Waqa were the core of traditional religion. Even more than the Oromo calendar, the Qalllu institution seems to have been profoundly influenced by ideas drawn from Islam. There are two reasons for making this conclusion. First and foremost, the national myths surrounding the origin of the first Qallu make them either of divine origin or the first son of Ilma Oromo (i.e., the oromo people).[16] However, there is sufficient evidence that the first Oromo high priests were of non-Oromo origin and that they were exposed to some rudimentary form of Islam.[17] The second reason deals with the story of Abba Muda, "the father" or the high priest for whom pilgrimage is made.[18] The term Muda, when used by itself is the name of the ceremony that is celebrated once every eight years in honor of the Qallu. The Muda ceremony was important because it was the point at which the Qallu institution and the Gada System intersected. "It is one of the critical foci of the Oromo polity."[19] According to Azaj Tino[20] one of the authors of the Chronicle of Emperor Susenyos (1607–1632), besides their belief in one Waqa (God), the Oromo believe in one single person whom they call Abba Muda and they all go to him from far and near to receive his blessings.[21] Those who went to Abba Muda and received his blessing and anointment were called jila and were considered "saints," the link between the spiritual father and the nation.[22]

The jila were considered "men of God," the concept that enlivened them with a "sacred quality," men without sin, a parallel concept with Muslim pilgrims to Sheikh Hussein of Bale or even to Mecca. On the route to the spiritual father, the jila were not molested even in enemy territory. On the contrary, the were given protection and the necessities of life. Their wives absented themselves from a number of things during their husbands' long journey, which in some cases took six months. The concept of ritual purity on the part of jila and their families seems to have parallels with the concept of "cleanliness," which is paramount among the Muslims who go to Mecca. In order to show their peaceful intentions they did not carry spears, the mark of manhood. Instead, they carried other insignia.

This had profound similarity to the pilgrimage to the tomb of Sheikh Hussein in Bale. The jila carried as a "badge" a forked stick, which they displayed on their way. The forked stick, we are told, had three branches standing for peace, unity, and knowledge of the ancient tradition. What is very striking is its similarity with the badge of those who even today go to Sheikh Hussein's tomb in Bale.[23]

I also suspect a cross-fertilization of ideas between the "benevolence" attributed to Sheikh Hussein and that of Abba Muda.[24] Hidden within this body of prayers chanted by the jila on the way to and from Abba Muda and by those who today go to Sheikh Hussein's tomb, it is possible to detect a common cultural source or tradition. I also find similarity between the traditional idea of generosity within Oromo society and the powerful image of Sheikh Hussein that inspires people to show kindness and charity to those pilgrims on their way to and from the tomb. In essence the latter is no different from the treatment the *jila* received in the past.[25] Abba Muda's "two hands" holding a blessing and a curse, the former so sought after, and the latter so dreaded, is not very different from the tradition of Sheikh Hussein.[26] Moreover, the isolated tomb of Sheikh Hussein in Bale does not seem to have suffered from the pastoral Oromo attacks during their epoch-making migration in the sixteenth century. Perhaps the tomb served as neutral ground for settling internal disputes among themselves and with their enemies.[27] This may have been due to Sheikh Hussein's influence on the Oromo through Abba Muda.

Finally, there is no doubt that the Oromo were exposed to Islamic influence even before their sixteenth century migration. Perhaps as early as the fourteenth, and certainly by the fifteenth century, the Islamic influence was filtering through into the area of the original home of the Oromo. The Islamic radiation out of historical Bali may have kindled a spark of Islam among the Oromo who lived within and on the periphery of the Medieval Christian Kingdom of Abyssinia. That spark may have burst into flame[28] during the short-lived *jihad* (holy war) of Imam Ahmad (1529–1543), popularly known as Ahmad Gran (the left-handed).

Islam as an Ideology of Resistance for the Oromo of Wallo, ca. 1700–1900

The region that later came to be known as Wallo

> commanded a pivotal position in North Central Ethiopia, it had served throughout the Medieval and early Modern period as a strategically indispensable route for conquests as well as retreats of regional and imperial levies.[29]

The fertility and the wealth of this region[30] served as an attraction for migration and settlement of both sedentary populations and pastoralists, including the Oromo.

Islam was established in Wallo before the sixteenth century. However, it was after the conquest of the region by Ahmad Gran in 1532, that the pre-existing Muslim communities were invigorated, a large number of people being converted to Islam through peaceful as well s violent means. As a result, new Muslim settlements were founded that "were to become instrumental in the further consolidation of Islam."[31] This means in Wallo, the Oromo pastoralists migrated into the region where Islam was well established.

The pastoral Oromo migration, which started before the *jihad* of Ahmad Gran (1529–1543), took considerable advantage of the situation crated hy that *jihad*. This was because the jihadic wars were disastrous for the defense of both the Christian kingdom and the Muslim state of Harar. The Christian military colonies in the southern provinces were dislodged by the jihadic wars. These military colonies had served as a powerful dam that minimized the overflow of the pastoral Oromo flood. The breakup of the dam at the most critical time was equally disastrous to both Muslims and Christians. Before the Christian kingdom fully recuperated and reestablished its military colonies in the southern provinces, the migrating Oromo displaced what was left after the jihadic wars and thwarted new attempts at settlement. Regions that had been sparsely populated before the *jihad*[32] were left empty by the shifting of population during the *jihad*. This explains why the Oromo easily overran huge areas in a short time.

It was in the last quarter of the sixteenth century that the Oromo migrated to and settled in the region of Wallo. Among the various groups who migrated and settled in Northern Ethiopia, the Yajju and the Wallo were the two most dominant. The yajju settled in the northern part of the medieval province of Amhara, where they established their own Muslim Yajju Dynasty, which dominated the political landscape of the Christian Kingdom of Gondar from 1756 to 1853. However, it was the Wallo group that gave its name to the region itself and formed a remarkable dynasty that used Islam as an ideology of resistance. Interestingly, of all the Oromo groups that settled in northern Ethiopia, the Wallo had a very strong Muslim tradition. This may be partly because they were the first to accept Islam. Even before their arrival in the norther region, some Wallow clans may have already embraced Islam. For instance, one of the seven clans of Wallo, Nole Warro Ali (Nole "the house of" Ali) seems to have been Muslim. Ali is an unmistakable Muslim name and usually only Muslim Oromo adopted Muslim names.

In Wallo, the Oromo settled among a large sedentary population, both Christians and Muslims. Surprisingly, the overwhelming majority of the Oromo embraced Islam. Why the Oromo rejected Christianity will become clearer further on in our discussion. Here it should suffice to say that in the course of several decades during the last part of the sixteenth century and the first half of the seventeenth century, the ground was prepared and the stage set for the transformation of the Oromo mode of production from pastoralism to sedentary agriculture, combined with cattle-keeping. There was also growth of trade, which was accompanied by the spread of Islam. This in turn set in motion a dynamic political process that eventually culminated in the birth of a new order represented by the Oromo states. In other words, by the second half of the seventeenth century, the Oromo in Wallo had already embraced Islam from the indigenous Muslim population of the region[33] and embarked on mixed farming, which became the dominant mode of their economy. It was not by accident that the first recorded account of a local Muslim Oromo dynasty, the Arreloch, was formed in Wallo during the second half of the seventeenth century.[34]

According to Trimingham, the Oromo in Wallo not only kept their identity but also "reinforced their independence by the adoption of Islam."[35] He goes on to add that the Oromo accepted Islam "as bulwark against being swamped by Abyssinian nationalism."[36] I indicated above that in Wallo the overwhelming majority of the Oromo embraced Islam. I must add that the Oromo did not reject Christianity as a religion, but the Abyssinian domination that preceded and followed the spread of Christianity. For the Oromo in Wallo, Abyssinian domination and Christianity were synonymous. As Christianity was one of the pillars of Abyssinian unity, Islam became a major unifying factor for the Oromo in Wallo. From the beginning, Islam for the Oromo in Wallo was part of their cultural life and a mark of their independence. It was a powerful symbol of their identity as a people and a reliable fortress against Abyssinian nationalism. From the perspectives of this discussion, the Oromo played a crucial role in the spread and consolidation of Islam in and beyond Wallo.

Their early Islamization, and their active role in the subsequent consolidation and expansion of Islam not only within their own cultural environment, but also in other areas under their domination such as Bagemder served to extend the reach of Islam. They helped to change the status of Islam from that of a religion of disparate communities to that of a dynastic ideology relevant to the entire region.[37]

Once the Muslim Oromo states were established in Wallo, Islam provided the rulers with a focus of unity transcending tribal loyalty. It also became an ideological weapon, a powerful arsenal with which "to combat the Christian Amhara territorial encroachment and cultural expansion."[38] Islam spread among the Oromo in Wallo during the after the seventeenth century. Its rapid success was explained by Trimingham in these terms:

> It was the religion hostile to that of the Amharic [sic] race who lorded it over them. . . . Amharic Christianity was fixed and sterile. The result was that as it had become more and more fossilized to embody the spirit and form of Ethiopian nationalism, it was regarded by pagan tribes as the tribal religion of their enemies. Islam, on the other hand, opening its arms to embrace all land sundry who cared to join its brother hood by the repetition of a simple formula, and accommodating as it was to their indigenous practices, also gave new converts pride of membership of a universal religious system transcending all racial barriers, whilst their incorporation into the system opened up to them possibilities of deeper religious experience. . .[39]

Of the six Muslim Oromo dynasties that came into existence in the region, today known as the province of Wallo, namely, the Arreloch, the Warra Himano, the Yajju, the Qallu, the house of the Gattiroch, and the Borana,[40] only the Warra Himano had a long history of championing the cause of Islam with more than usual vigor and dynamism, resisting Christian territorial encroachment and cultural expansion with creative dynamism and ingenuity. It was this resistance that exhibited the heroism of the Muslim population in Wallo, demonstrated the strength of Islamic establishment in the region, and constituted the glorious chapter of the history the Warra Himano Dynasty.

The Imamate of Warra Himano

The Warra Himano Dynasty (ca. 1700–1916) was the second Muslim Oromo dynasty to be established in Wallo, the first to declare a *jihad* in the name and interest of Islam, the first to adopt the prestigious title of Imam, and the longest surviving dynasty in the region. The original founder of the dynasty was a wealthy Muslim cleric named Godana Babbo, who migrated with his small Muslim Oromo group from Arsi, in southern Ethiopia, towards the end of the seventeenth century and settled at Garfa, in Wallo. The migration of this Muslim Oromo group suggests that Islam had already begun to spread among the Oromo in Arsi even during the seventeenth century. Godana used his Islamic knowledge and wealth for establishing his power and spreading his fame far and wide. From Garfa, his power base, Godana expanded his territorial control and political influence "over the surrounding indigenous populations," thus laying "the foundation for a Muslim dynasty that was to last for nearly two hundred years."[41] In the words of a promising brilliant young scholar, on whose work this chapter has heavily drawn:

> . . . Godana's success in wielding power and in founding a hereditary ruling dynasty is an exceptional case of a Muslim cleric exploiting his credentials as a religious notable to achieve a political objective. It also explains why his later successors inherited his religious fervor and commitment. It thus demonstrated that Islam has been used as an ideology for building up a local power based and for pursuing a policy of territorial expansion.[42]

Godana's successors continued with their territorial expansion and consolidation, which reached its zenith during the reign of Muhammad Ali (ca. 1771–1785), who was a farsighted leader, a resourceful politician, and a fervent Muslim. Farsighted because he realized that Christian victory would entail not only a loss of independence for his kingdom but would also force conversion to Christianity. Resourceful because he continued to resist the superior imperial force even after he was defeated. And fervent because he appointed notable religious men to positions of power and authority and "attempted through them to eradicate certain vestiges of animist worship, practices and traditional customary laws."[43] It was during his reign that some aspects of Islamic law, the Shari'a, began to influence the lives of the people, "as he sought to make the Shari'a the basis of the prevailing legal system." It appears that in matters of marriage and inheritance the Shari'a replaced traditional Oromo law. Muhammad Ali "used Islam as a basis for consolidating his power by seeking and obtaining the support and the sanction of the Muslim scholars and jurists."[44] He realized the importance of uniting all Oromo leaders in Wallo under a single central administration for the purpose of facing the challenge from Emperor Takla Giyorgis. In the fierce battle of Legot in March 1783, Muhammad Ali was defeated by Takla Giyorgis. However, it was a pyrrhic victory as the former went on, not only resisting the latter but also succeeding in establishing his power over wider territory.[45]

Muhammad Ali died in 1785 and was succeeded by his son Batto (1785–1790), who was coerced by the Emperor to embrace Christianity. This was a major setback for Islam and for the dynasty that championed it. However, the setback was shortlived as Batto's successor Amade (1790–1803) was a fervent Muslim. Amade was a very energetic and capable leader who mobilized his forces and, in a dramatic move, he undertook a military expedition precisely to avenge his predecessor's forced conversion to Christianity.[46] In 1798, Amade even occupied the imperial city of Gondar, put his own puppet nominee on the Christian throne, and "had the call to the Muslim prayer announced from the tower of one of the castles in Gondar, as a symbolic gesture of his triumphal entry into the city, and perhaps to emphasize his religious zeal."[47] Undoubtedly Amade did much to strengthen the position of Islam in and beyond Wallo, and that religion in turn strengthened and sanctified the hereditary power of his dynasty in Wallo. It is reported that Amade "obtained a formal authority from Mecca that permitted him and his descendants to assume the honorific title of Imam."[48]

Imam Amade died in 1803 and was succeeded by Imam Liban (1803–1815), who died while fighting for the Islamic cause and was succeeded by Imam Amade II (1815–1838), who is reported to have asked Muhammad Ali (1805–1848) of Egypt for his collaboration in conquering and converting Northern Ethiopia.[49] Imam Amade was the regent to the young Ras Ali II (1831–53) of the Yajju dynasty, who was the real power behind the Christian throne in Gondar. Thus Amade wielded enormous power, and it was during his reign that the Oromo of Wallo became the "most active centre of Muslim propaganda in East Africa,"[50] and Islam reached its zenith in northern Ethiopia. Amade, a zealous Muslim, "was considered by many the most important Muslim ruler, if not the leader of all the Muslims of Ethiopia."[51] Given that, the triumph of Islam in Northern Ethiopia might have been expected to be more sure, swift, and lasting. However, this failed to material-ize, with disastrous consequences for the Muslims in Northern Ethiopia, for (among others) three interrelated factors: the rivalry among Oromo leaders, the arrival of Europeans on the scene, and above all the revival of Christian nationalism in historic Abyssinia.

Imam amade II died in 1838, and was succeeded by Imam Liban (1838–41), another fervent Muslim leader whose removal from power by Ras Ali Ii unleashed an intense power struggle among the Oromo leaders of Wallo, which in turn led to the challenge and gradual weakening of the preponder-ant position of Islam in northern Ethiopia. While the Oromo strength was consumed with their own quarrels, their enemies rejoiced in the important discovery of the weakness of the internal dissension of Oromo leaders. Oromo weakness was the blessing in disguise for the Amhara leaders of Bagemder and Shawa who did everything possible to turn Oromo leaders against one another "in order to secure local allies who would be amenable to the expansion of their sphere of influence."[52] The division among the Oromo leaders widened in the 1840s and 1850s, and it fortuitously coincided with the change in the balance of power in favor of the Christian polity and the revival of Abyssinian nationalism. The change in the balance of power was brought about primarily due to the arrival of European missionaries, traders, diplomats, adventurers, and mercenaries, who facilitated the importation of modern European weapons of destruction into northern Ethiopia. European missionaries who "tended to relate the success of their own cause to political support for the ambitions of the indigenous Christian polities"[53] provided ideological justification for supporting the Christians in Abyssinia. "For the sake of Christianity and civilization, these Christians in Africa have to be helped. To help them is to destroy Islam and strengthen Christianity."[54] So it was in the 1850s when the clouds had already gathered thick and low over the once formidable Oromo cavalry in Wallo that the revival of Abyssinian Christian nationalism consolidated itself.

Emperor Tewodros (1855–1868) and Wallo

Tewodros expressed and represented the revival of Abyssinian nationalism in its crude form. He had three interrelated goals: to break the power of the Oromo leaders of Wallo and destroy them, to make a frontal assault on Islam with combined forces of the resurgent state and the church; and to convert or expel all other Muslims from his land. For Tewodros "Christianity and Abyssinia were synonymous."[55] Tewodros fleetingly united historical Abyssinia on clearly stated anti-Oromo and anti-Islamic policies which were:

> supported by the contemporary protestant missionaries for three reasons: firstly, because they hoped that the subjugation of Wallo would inaugurate a period of tranquility; secondly, because they saw the struggle in terms of a confrontation between Christianity and Islam; and thirdly, because they believed that Wallo was the spearhead of the Muslim drive to take over Ethiopia.[56]

For Tewodros, Wallo and Islam were synonymous. As an emperor who called himself "the slave of Christ,"[57] it was his religious and political duty to destroy Wallo and Islam. This perhaps explains his intense hatred of Islam and his inhuman devastation of Wallo.

Shortly after his coronation in 1855, Tewodros marched to Wallo and fought against three rival Oromo leaders, killing one, capturing the second, and defeating the third. For the next ten years Tewodros marched several times into Wallo, devastating, burning, looting, and massacring the people. Violent terrorism characterized his campaigns in Wallo.[58] And yet Tewodros was never able to crush the resistance of the Muslim population in Wallo. The reasons for the tenacious Muslim resistance were:

> Firstly, Tewodros's policy of indiscriminate devastation and destruction of the land and the deportation of some of the people; and secondly, his clearly anti-Muslim, and even anti-Oromo, stance. The leaders of the rebellion perceived Tewodros' objectives and activities as being directed not only to destroying them as a ruling class, but also to undermining the social, economic and cultural foundation of the Muslim communities themselves.[59]

Encouraged by European Protestant missionary support, intoxicated by his ravenous ambition to destroy Islam and the Oromo power, and surprised by the tenacious Muslim resistance, Tewodros spent more than ten years destroying Wallo, by which he too was destroyed. The Muslims of Wallo, united by danter and animated by Islam, resisted Tewodros bravely before he was overwhelmed by crisis and destroyed. Hence,

> as far as his stated aim of forcing Muslim Oromo into either accept-[ing] Christianity or leav[ing] his kingdom, he utterly failed. He, not they, gave in. It is not an exaggeration to say that Tewodros commit-ted suicide in 1868, not only because he hated to fall into British hands as a captive king, but also because he was already virtually an Oromo prisoner in the mountain fortress of Magdala. Escape was well neigh impossible.[60]

Nevertheless, Tewodros's anti-Islam and anti-Oromo stance[61] affected the future resistance of Warro in two ways. First, "the extent of physical and material destruction and pillaging of the Wallo countryside affected the demographic, economic and political vitality of the region for the remaining part of the century."[62] Secondly, he instituted a policy to physically destroying Muslim leaders. His policy, in fact, became the working model for his successors, Emperors Yohannes and Menilek, based as it was upon the elimination or conversion of Oromo leaders, the destruction of the mosques, and the complete subjugation of the Muslims to the Christian Amhara political, economic, cultural, and social domination.

Emperor Yohannes IV (1872–1889): Policy Towards Islam and the Muslim Resistance in Wallo

During the reign of Tewodros (1855–1868), though united resistance was lacking, individual dynastic resistance, spearheaded by the imamate of Warra Himano, was very impressive. It was this tenacious resistance that prevented Tewodros from realizing his goals of uprooting Islam and destroying Oromo power in Wallo. After the death of Tewodros, it must be noted that the Oromo leaders of Wallo had learned nothing from their past mistakes, nor did they forget their rivalry. On the contrary, their rivalry intensified, being freshly fueled by the intrigues of the Christian war lords and the strong ambition of Menilek, the Amhara king of Shawa (1865–1889) and later the Emperor of Ethiopia (1889–1913). From the beginning Menilek wanted to expand the northern frontier of his kingdom at the expense of Wallo. Out of the intense power struggle in Wallo, there emerged Imam Muhammad Ali and Imam Abba Wataw, "two young representatives of the rival factions of the Warra Himano ruling clan."[63] It is important to note here that in their struggle against the Christians, the ruling family of the Warra Himano was united. In fact, internal unity was the strength of the dynasty. The basic goal of the leaders of Warra Himano was simple and their vision clear: to defend Islam and to preserve the independence of Wallo. During the reign of Yohannes, the people hoped that their leaders would strengthen their unity and inspire them to resist the Abyssinian assault with vigor. To their great disappointment Imam Muhammad Ali and Imam Abba Wataw forgot their responsibility to their people and to the survival of Islam and remembered only factional interests, inadvertently inflicting wounds on Wallo. The irony of the history of the Warra Himano dynasty was that it lost internal unity when it most needed to defend Islam. Thus the Warra Himano dynasty lacked a single leader capable of mobilizing the people, marshalling their resources, and galvanizing them into action with a singleness of purpose and determination. The two feuding leaders fought more with each other than with their common enemy. This division within the Muslim leadership in Wallo created an ideal condition that provided Menilek of Shawa with both the incentive for conquest and the relative ease with which that conquest would be accomplished between 1868 and 1876, by which time most of Wallo was under the control of Menilek.

In other words, the futile power struggle in which neither of the two leaders gained his objective, but inadvertently contributed to the decline of Wallo, fortuitously coincided with the dramatic rising power of Yohannes of Tigray and Menilek of Shawa. These two rival Christian princes met at Boru Meda in Wallo in May or June 1878, and issued a most ominous edict, which demanded that all Muslims had to convert to Christianity. The edict:

> contains an explicit reference to a historical fact: the devastation of Christian territory under Gran [1529–1543] who had forcibly converted the people to Islam—and hence a spirit of Christian vengeance can be seen lurking behind the formulation of the edict. . . . The edict also obligated the recalcitrant to leave the land since 'Muslims have no country.'[64]

After the Council of 1878, Imam Muhammad Ali and Imam Abba Wataw were converted to Christianity: "The former took the baptismal name, Mekael and his godfather was Yohannes," while the latter became Hayla Maryam and his godfather was Menilek.[65] The Warra Himano dynasty that made Islam an ideology of resistance for over a century and made its name and fame in defending Islam, abandoned its historical role with the conversion of the two erstwhile rival members of the dynasty. But that did not mark the end of Muslim resistance in Wallo. On the contrary, the resistance continued under militant clerics with much more vigor, vitality, and intensity. In fact, the conversion of the two principal leaders:

> marked a turning point in the long history of Wallo resistance against imperial policy of subjugation which had been led by the hereditary chiefs of the region. From the time of the conversion of the two principal representatives of the Warra Himano ruling family, the opposition was to be pre-eminently led by Muslim militant clerics.[66]

Emperor Yohannes, who was determined to obtain unity in northern Ethiopia, "masquerading under a religious guise,"[67] officially banned Islam in 1879, the ban that lasted for decade characterized by tremendous loss of life and wanton property destruction in Wallo. It was the irony of history that Menilek who escaped from Tewodros' prison in 1865, gaining the throne of Shawa with the support of Wallo Oromo, now joined with Yohannes for their destruction! The two principal Christian princes were quick to take cruel revenge on the Muslims who refused to convert, and that revenge reached its climax in the 1880s, at the time when European-supplied weapons of destruction enabled Yohannes and Menilek to create the most formidable military machine in Africa. As in the days of Tewodros, massacre, plunder, burning, looting, and wanton destruction of property became the lot of Muslims in Wallo. In this revenge of history, it was not so much the events of the last quarter of the nineteenth century that seemed to reassert themselves but the ferocious spirit of the era of jihadic war of Imam Ahmad (1529–1543). Tewodros, Yohannes, and Menilek seemed to be looking back angrily to the time of Ahmad Gran, when their forefathers were defeated, and for which they indulged in a revenge of history while devastating Wallo. Wallo was divided into two parts, and the northern part came under the control of Yohannes, while the southern part came under the control of Menilek. All over Wallo, Muslim schools were closed and mosques turned into churches. In every aspect—religious, cultural, economic, political, and military—the Muslims in Wallo were attacked from the north by Yohannes and from the south by Menilek.

In 1879, Yohannes ravaged Yajju and Rayya in the Wallo region, killing many *ulama* and jurists who refused to convert. Again in 1880, Yohannes ravaged Yajju and many places including Qallu,

> where his troops committed more excesses than in any other place. The reason was that Qallu was renowned as an active centre of Islamic learning and propagation and the home of famous Muslim scholars. . . [He] founded new churches and ordered the mass baptism of the [Muslims]. He also instructed . . . Menilek to collect and burn all Muslim books. In 1881, 1882 and 1884 [Yohannes] and Menilek ravaged Qallu and [killed numerous religious leaders]. . . In early 1886 about 20,000 men and women who refused to abjure their loyalty to Islam were massacred . . . in Qallu.[68]

Muslim resistance against the combined forces of Yohannes and Menilek was led by militant religious leaders. What turned Muslim clerics into militant leaders of rebellion was intimately connected with the total assault on Islam. Indeed, the outrage committed against Islam, Muslim institutions of learning, the mosques, and the Muslim population may have galvanized the Muslim clerics into spontaneous resistance. Many died resisting with weapons in their hands rather than witness the destruction of their Muslim heritage. Deprived of their religious and political rights, and reduced to landless *gebbars* (serfs) in the land of their birth, the Muslims of Wallo had no choice but to reembark on the road of resistance. By resisting, they had nothing to lose but a great deal to gain. There were a number of militant Muslim religious leaders who led armed opposition against both Yohannes and Menilek. However, the most famous was the Sheikh Talhah, who put up a heroic resistance against both Yohannes and Menilek. He was born around 1850 to a family noted for its Islamic education. He received many years of religious training both in Dawway and in Qallu, the two most famous centers of learning in Wallo. He was a distinguished teacher, a celebrated organizer, and a brilliant and resourceful leader. Sheikh Talhah declared *jihad* in 1884 and initially "achieved spectacular success by inflicting devastating losses in men and property upon the forces of Yohannes's commanders."[69] For many months, he eluded capture, recovered from serious defeats, and was exceptionally resourceful in extricating himself from the most difficult situations. Outnumbered and outgunned, he was driven out of Wallo and went to the Sudan, where he established political and military alliances with the leaders of the Mahdist state. Later he returned to Wallo and registered a proud heritage of resistance.[70] However, because of the vast superiority of the Christian force, Sheikh Talhah's *jahid* failed to achieve its objective. This brings us to the fundamental question: Was the Muslim resistance in Wallo a failure? The short and objective answer is that militarily it was indeed a failure. However, there are four areas in which the resistance achieved some success. First,

> The resistance can be said to have played some role not only in tying down the forces of the Christian rulers who were determined [to convert all Muslims] but also in harassing Christian garrisons and clergy sent to look after the new converts . . . thus minimizing the likelihood of a thorough conversion. [Second and] just as importantly, the militant opposition also directly influenced the policy of Yohannes's successor, Menilek, who in 1889 restored freedom of worship.[71]

Third, the Muslim resistance in Wallo in fact made a remarkable contribution to the spread of Islam in the southeast and southwestern parts of Ethiopia. How did this come about? The enforced conversion in Wallo led to the exodus of a large number of people, including the *ulama* and jurist, to the southeast and southwestern parts of Ethiopia. Many fled to the Sudan and the Hijaz.[72] Those who fled to the southeast went to the Charchar region of Hararghe, where they settled among the Oromo and "found new diffusion centers for Islam."[73] Those who fled to the southwest settled mainly in the Oromo states in the Gibe region. Many *ulama* and jurists settled in the

Kingdom of Jimma, where shortly after their arrival, sixty *madras* (schools of higher education) were established.[74] In this sense the fugitive scholars from Wallo made unique contribution to the flowering of Muslim education so much so that Jimma became the second most famous center of Islamic learning for all Oromo of Ethiopia. Even today, along with Dawwey in Wallo, Jimma is regarded as the best center of Islamic learning in the Horn of Africa.[75]

Fourth, the Muslim resistance in Wallo seems also to have led to the growth of a jihadic movement in the Gibe region. The Muslim clerics who made Islam the religion of the masses and nurtured Islamic culture in Wallo, brought the spirit of resistance with them to the Gibe region. This spirit of resistance grew into a jihadic movement mainly in the Kingdom of Gumma, which remained the hotbed of rebellion and Muslim resistance from 1887 to 1902.[76]

Finally, the above necessarily incomplete account of Muslim resistance in Wallo "provides an insight into and throws a considerable light on" the interaction between the expansion of the Christian Ethiopian state and the Oromo response to that phenomena. For the Oromo of Wallo, Islam was an ideology of resistance, a powerful arsenal behind their tenacious moral will to endure incredible hardship. In the exodus of Muslim *ulama* and jurists from Wallo in the 1880s, it is possible to perceive the enduring vigor and vitality of Islamic establishment in Wallo, the militancy of the religious leaders, the range and diversity of their initiative, and the extent to which they went to save Islam and the Muslim community from destruction in and beyond Wallo.

Notes

1. Mekuria Bulcha, "Onesimos Nasib's Pioneering Contributions to Oromo Literature." Paper presented at the Second International Symposium on Cushitic and Omotic Languages, Turin, 16–18 November 1989, p. 1. I am indebted to the author for giving me a copy of this paper.
2. Gene Gragg, *Oromo Dictionary*. East Lansing, Michigan: Michigan State University

1982.

3. Darrel Bates, *The Abyssinian Difficulties: The Emperor Theodorus and the Magdala Campaign 1867–68.* Oxford: 1979, p. 7.

4. When reference is made to Bali, it means the historical province and when the reference is made to Bale, it means the present administrative region of the same name.

5. E. Haberland, *Galla-sud Athiopiens.* Stuttgart: Kohlhammer, 1963, p. 772.

6. Mohammed Hasses, *The Oromo of Ethiopia: A History 1570–1860.* Cambridge: Cambridge University press, 1990, p. 4. See also Haberland, *Ibid.,* p. 774.

7. The one exception is M. Abir, "Ethiopia and the Horn of Africa" in *Cambridge History of Africa, Volume 4, From c. 1600 to c. 1790,* edited by Richard Gray. Cambridge: Cambridge University Press, 1978, p. 552.

8. J. S. Trimingham, *Islam in Ethiopia.* Oxford: Oxford University Press, 1952, p. 198.

9. See, for instance, Taddesse Tamrat, *Church and State in Ethiopia 1270–1527.* Oxford: Oxford University Press, 1972, pp. 73–4, 95 *et passim.*

10. This, of course, does not mean that there is no variation in the calendar. Indeed, there are variations in the names of the months, and changing seasons of the year both in the highlands and lowlands. And yet, the core of the calendar from East to West, North to South is the same.

11. Asmarom Legesse, *Gada: Three Approaches to the Study of African Society.* London: 1973, p. 279.

12. Haberland, *Ibid.,* p. 777.

13. Legesse, *Ibid.,* p. 278–282.

14. Mohammed Hassen, "The Oromo of Ethiopia, 1500–1850: With Special Emphasis on the Gibe Region." Ph.D. Dissertation, University of London, 1983, pp. 96–100. See also Sefu Metaferia, "The Eastern Oromo (Kottu) of Ethiopia and Their Time Reckoning System." *Africa Rivista trimistrale di Studi e Documentozione Dell'Instituto Italo-Africano,* Vol. XXXIII, No. 4 (1978), pp. 475–507.

15. Legesse, *Ibid.,* p. 279.

16. See for instance, K. Knutsson, *Authority and Change: A Study of the Kallu Institution Among the Macha Galla of Ethiopia.* Goteborg: 1967, pp. 145–7. See also Paul Baxter, "Social Organization of the Galla of Northern Kenya." D. Phil. Disserta-

tion, Oxford University, 1954, pp. 156–192; Haberland, *Galla Sud-Athiopiens*, pp. 475, 537; and Martial de Salviac, *Un peuple antique au pays de Menelik: Les Galla Grande Nation Africane*. Paris: 1905, p. 152.

17. Mohammed Hassen, "The Oromo of Ethiopia," *Ibid.*, p. 110. See also Ulrich Braukamper, "Islamic Principalities in Southeast Ethiopia Between the 13th and 16th Centuries," *Ethiopianist Notes*, Vol. I, No. 2 (1977), pp. 27–28.

18. Because anointment with butter was one of his important blessings some writers have tended to translate Abba Muda as the father of anointment. See for instance, G.W.B. Huntingford, *The Galla of Ethiopia: The Kingdom of Kafa and Janjero*. International African Institute, London: 1955, p. 83.

19. Legesse, *Gada, Ibid.*, p. 216.

20. Azaj Tino, himself was of Oromo origin. He was converted to Catholicism in 1622 together with Emperor Susenyos.

21. F. M. Pereira, *Chronica de Susenvos Rei di Ethiopie*. Lisbon: 1892, p. 214.

22. Angelo Mizzi, *Anni etnografici Galla ossia organizzaione civile use e costumi Oromonici*. Malta: 1935, p. 9. See also de Salviac, *Les Galla, Ibid.*, 152, 155–56.

23. See, for instance, E. Cerulli, *Ethiopia Occidentale*, Vol. II. Roma: 1933, p. 145 and J. S. Trimingham, *Islam in Ethiopia*, p. 250.

24. B. W. Andrzejewski, "Sheikh Hussen of Bali in Galla Oral Traditions," in *IV Congresso Internazionale di studi Etiopici*. Roma: 1974, pp. 33–34.

25. De Salviac, *Les Galla*, pp. 157–58.

26. Anonymous, *Rabi-al-Qulub*. Cairo: 1927, pp. 13–23 et passim. This is an Arabic book that deals with the life history and miracles of Sheikh Hussein of Bale.

27. See, for instance, R. A. Caulk, "Harar Town and Its Neighbors in the Nineteenth Century," in *The Journal of African History*, Vol XVIII (1977), p. 372.

28. This means that some Oromo groups may have already accepted Islam even before their sixteenth century migration. Some evidence to be presented below supports this conclusion.

29. Hussein Ahmed, "Clerics, Traders and Chiefs: A Historical Study of Islam in Wallo (Ethiopia) with Special Emphasis on the Nineteenth Century." Ph.D. Dissertation, University of Birmingham, 1986, p. 82.

30. Francisco Alveres, *The Prester John of the Indies*, eds. C.F. Beckingham and G.W.B. Huntingford. Cambridge: 1961, Vol. I. p. 338.

31. Hussein Ahmed, *Ibid.*, p. 97, 165.
32. J. A. Davis, "The Sixteenth Century Jihad in Ethiopia and the Impact on its Culture," in *Journal of the Historical Society of Nigeria*, Vol. III (1964), p. 113.
33. Trimingham, *Islam in Ethiopia*, p. 193.
34. Zergaw Asfera, "Some Aspects of Historical Development in Amhara (Wallo), ca. 1700–1815," B.A. Thesis, Addis Ababa University, 1973, pp. 10–16.
35. Trimingham, *Ibid.*, p. 107.
36. *Ibid.*, p. 109.
37. Hussein Ahmed, *Ibid.*, p. 119. See also Trimingham, *Ibid.*, pp. 106, 110–11 and M. Abir, *Ethiopia: The Era of the Prices, the Challenge of Islam and the Reunification of the Christian Empire 1769–1955*. London: Longman, Green & Co., Limited, 1968, p. 113.
38. Hussein Ahmed, *Ibid.*, pp. 154–55. See also Trimingham, *Ibid.*, pp. 101 and E. Cerulli, "L'Islam en Ethiopie: sa signification historique et ses methodes," *Correspondence d'Orient* 5 (1961), p. 319.
39. Trimingham, *Ibid.*, pp. 101–102.
40. Hussein Ahmed, *Ibid.*, pp. 268–272.
41. *Ibid.*, pp. 118, 254–256.
42. *Ibid.*, p. 256.
43. *Ibid.*, p. 261.
44. *Ibid.*
45. *Ibid.*, pp. 159–61. See also M. Abir, "Ethiopia and the Horn of Africa" in *Cambridge History of Africa*, Vol. 4, ed. Richard Gray. Cambridge: Cambridge University Press, 1975, p. 573.
46. Hussein Ahmed, *Ibid.*, p. 205.
47. *Ibid.*, p. 264.
48. *Ibid.*, p. 265.
49. *Ibid.*, p. 266. See also M. Abir, *Ethiopia: The Era of the Princes.* pp. 105, 114–15, 117.
50. Arnauld d'Abbadie, *Douze ans de Sijour dans la haute-Ethiopie (Abyssinie)*. Ed., Jeanne-Marie Allier. Vatican: 1980, Vol. II, pp. 200–201. Translation by Hussein Ahmed, *Ibid.*, p. 273.
51. M. Abir, *Ethiopia: The Era of the Princes*, p. 33.

52. Hussein Ahmed, *Ibid.*, p. 272. See also A. D'Abbadie, *Ibid.*, p. 200.

53. Richard Greenfield and Mohammed Hassen, "Interpretation of Oromo Nationality," in *Horn of Africa*, Vol. III, No. 3 (1980), p. 6.

54. "Afrique Memoirs et Documente Abyssinia, 1938–1850," in *Archives des Afraires Etrangers*. Paris, Vol. I, No. 13, Folio 129–130.

55. Trimingham, *Islam in Ethiopia*, p. 118.

56. Hussein Ahmed, "Clerics, Traders, and Chiefs," p. 331, citing Donald Crummey, "Tewodros as Reformer, and Modernizer," in *Journal of African History*, X, 3 (1969), pp. 466–67.

57. Hussein Ahmed, *Ibid.*, p. 329.

58. Donald Crummey, "The Violence of Tewodros" in *War and Society in Africa*, ed., A. Ogot. London: Longman, 1972, p. 68.

59. Hussein Ahmed, *Ibid.*, p. 329.

60. Richard Greenfield and Mohammed Hassen, "Interpretation of Oromo Nationality," *Horn of Africa*, p. 8.

61. It is said that Tewodros's anti-Oromo stance survived to his last life breath. At the last minute of his life Tewodros released all the prisoners in Magdala except the Wallo and Shawa Oromo numbering about 1,000. He killed all Oromo prisoners; not even a single person escaped his massacre. (Waldhansso, *Journal of the Union of Oromo Students in North America*, 1979, pp. 19–20.

62. Hussein Ahmed, *Ibid.*, p. 333. See also Donald Crummey, "The Violence of Tewodros," pp. 66, 76.

63. *Ibid.*, p. 336.

64. *Ibid.*, p. 338. See also Richard A. Caulk, "Religion and the State in Nineteenth Century Ethiopia," in *Journal of Ethiopian Studies*, Vol. X, No. 1 (1972), p. 32.

65. Hussein Admed, *Ibid.*, p. 344. See also Harold G. Marcus, *The Life and Times of Menilek II: Ethiopia 1844–1913*. Oxford: Oxford University Press, 1975, p. 58.

66. *Ibid.* See also Fekadu Begna, "A Tentative History of Wallo, 1855–1908," B.A. Thesis, Addis Ababa University, 1972, p. 44.

67. Trimingham, *Islam in Ethiopia*, p. 123.

68. Hussein Ahmed, *Ibid.*, pp. 346 See also R. A. Caulk, "Religion and the State," p. 29. Fekadu Begna, *Ibid.*, p. 45.

69. *Ibid.*, p. 45.

70. According to Hussein Ahmed, *Ibid.*, p. 354:

   > After the death of Yohannes in 1889 Sahykh Talhah continued to defy Menilek even after the edict of 1878 had been officially rescinded. He died in . . . 1936, after a remarkable though turbulent life.

71. *Ibid.*, p. 360.
72. *Ibid.*, p. 356.
73. Trimingham, *Islam in Ethiopia*, p. 123.
74. The Manuscript of Abba Jobir Abba Dala, the last King of Jimma, p. 11.
75. Mohammed Hassen, *The Oromo of Ethiopia: A History 1570–1860*, pp. 158–9.
76. *Ibid.*, p. 160. See also E. Cerulli, *Folk-Literature of the Galla of Southern Abyssinia*, Harvard African Studies 3 (1922), pp. 46, 52.

CHAPTER FIVE

Popular Islam in Twentieth-Century Africa

The Muslims of Gondar, 1900–1935[1]

ABDUSAMAD AHMAD

ETHIOPIA HAD A HISTORIC ISLAMIC community. Yet both Ethiopian and foreign historians tend to view Ethiopia as a Christian country. If they are at all conscious of Islam in Ethiopia, they see it as a geographically distinct and politically marginal phenomenon. In this view Ethiopia consists firstly of a solid dominant block of Christians who live in the highland plateaus and secondly of disparate groups of pastoral lowlanders who follow Islam. The history of Ethiopia then becomes in part the account of tensions and conflicts between these two elements. There are many inadequacies in this view. This study seeks to correct the one concerning the religiously monolithic character of the highlands.

While it is true that the highlands were dominated by Christianity, it is equally true that the highlands possessed a permanent, indigenous Muslim minority, a minority whose native language was either Tegrenna or Amharic.

As was so frequently the case elsewhere in Africa, the ongoing life of the highland Ethiopian Muslims was closely connected to trade. My concern in this article is to demonstrate the relative economic importance and the survival of the few Gondarine Muslims amidst the majority Christians, who looked at their mercantile job with contempt and considered their religion inferior.

From the middle of the eighth century onwards, Muslim Arabs began to control the Red Sea and to close the contact between Ethiopia's Christians and their co-religionists in the Byzantine empire. Internally, Christian power came to concentrate on the Ethiopian highlands. Meanwhile, Islam entered Ethiopia associating itself in the beginning with trade and nomadic life on the coastal lowlands. Muslim traders from the lowlands soon began to operate freely throughout the highland areas.[2] The Ethiopian nobility and the Muslim merchants needed one another. The Muslims needed direct contact with the Sidama lands to the south of the Blue Nile, which were the sources of the most valuable commodities involved in the long distance trade. These commodities included slaves, civet, wax, honey, gold and coffee. For their part Ethiopian rulers needed Muslim merchants to bring them foreign commodities such as silk and linen cloth, carpets, and the like.

With trade, Islam spread into the highlands. Late in the first millennium, the institutions of the highland kingdom had become thoroughly Christian-ized. Many peasants had adopted Christianity as their religion. However, some highlanders had begun to profess Islam. Those who embraced Islam became territorially segregated from and socially ostracized by their Christian neighbors and rulers.

Tadesse Tamrat has provided an excellent overview of medieval Ethiopia, when the empire was ruled by the so-called Solomonic emperors from their restoration in 1270 to their eclipse in 1527.[3] However, he pays little attention to Islam as a subject in itself and ignores the existence of the Muslim minority within the so-called Christian highlands.

Edward Ullendorff continues the story and gives brief information about Christian-Muslim relations in the subsequent period. He draws attention to the great *jihad* (holy war) of Ahmed ibn Ibrahim (nicknamed Gran), who had strengthened his position in Adal and became master of what is now south-eastern Ethiopia. From 1529 to 1543, Gran dominated the so-called Christian highlands. His *jihad* got a ready reply from the discontented elements, who were opposed to the expansion of Amhara soldiers from the Christian highlands, during the reign of Amda Siyon (1312–42) and his successors. Ullendorff views Gran's *jihad* as having reinforced superficial conversion to Islam.[4] If the conversion to Islam was as superficial as Ullendorff would like us to believe, why did the minority Muslims in the so-called Christian highlands continue to profess Islam even after the death of Gran in 1543? Ullendorff also fails to draw our attention to the recurring theme in the chronicle of Galawdewos, who ascended the throne following the upheaval brought about by Gran. This recurring theme was what we might call a Christian *jihad*, which ravaged the Muslim territories of present-day south-eastern Ethiopia.[5] Unlike Taddesse Tamrat's account, Ullendorff's is partisan. Moreover, he does not illuminate the origin of the Muslim community with which I am concerned: the Muslims of Gondar.

The founding of Gondar as the imperial capital, during the reign of Fasiladas (1632–67) coincided with the return of peace for a kingdom wracked for a hundred years by warfare and rebellion. The return of peace favored the expansion of trade, and Gondar emerged probably as Ethiopia's first true urban center.[6] This is clear from an account of a journey to Gondar by the Yemeni Qadi Sharaf al-Din al-Hassan. In response to this visit in 1642, Fasiladas sent an embassy to Yemen to negotiate the trade relations of Ethiopia and Yemen.[7] Some five years later, in 1647, he sent a second embassy to Yemen. This time he sent an Ethiopian Muslim by the name of al-hajj Salim b. 'Abd al-Rahim and a Christian whose name was not men-tioned. The expansion of trade apparently favored the Muslims, who were a significant component of the town's population,[8] and were described as having been rich.[9] This gave impetus to the development of commercial activities throughout the highlands.[10]

By contrast, the Christian aristocrats and their lesser officials devoted themselves to four professions: i.e., government, soldiery, priesthood, and farming. Thus, the rulers and the common people generally looked on mercantile activity with contempt. Yet, such an attitude did not fully exclude Christians from commercial activities. Alongside their Muslim peers, there were many well-established Christian merchants throughout the highlands. So, while Muslims were generally restricted to trade and generally dominated that activity, they did not monopolize it.

Fasiladas's son Yohannis I, (1667–82) known as "the Just," made no attempt to pursue his father's foreign policy in relation to Muslims. In fact, he was preoccupied with many religious questions.[11] Accordingly, he called a council at Gondar. The promulgation of the Church Council of Gondar in 1668 affected all religious minorities. The Franks (descendants of the Portuguese who came to support Galawdewos in the sixteenth century in his war with Ahmad Gran) were asked to leave, or else to profess the local monophysite christianity. The Falashas or black Jews were also subjected to territorial segregation and inferior status. The Muslims were assigned to live in the territorially segregated, lower quarter of the town on the banks of the Qaha river.[12] This Muslim quarter was called Beit al-Islam in Arabic, or Islam Bet in Amharic.[13]

From 1668 to 1698, thirty years elapsed before we gain fresh information of Gondar's Muslims. In 1698, the French traveller Charles Jacques Poncet visited Gondar and wrote about the mercantile activity of its Muslims.[14] The chronicles of Iyassu II and Iyo'as, edited by Guidi, do not mention the activity of the Gondarine Muslims.[15] Seventy-one years after Poncet's visit, we have another external observer in 1769 with the coming of the Scottish traveller James Bruce, who reached Gondar by way of Egypt and the Sudan. Bruce estimated that there were about three thousand Muslim houses there, some of which were spacious and good.[16]

The Muslims of Gondar, like their co-religionists elsewhere in the Ethiopian highlands, were originally peasants. My informants recount that most Muslims at one unspecified time were proprietors of land. Some Muslims came as immigrants from Tigrai, and coastal lands of Eritrea following the trade routes from Massawa to Gondar. These Muslim merchants spread Islam to the neighboring villages ever since they began to operate trade freely throughout the Ethiopian highlands from the middle of the eighth century onwards. The villagers near and around Gondar who accepted Islam were denied land-holding rights and therefore pursued trade and crafts to maintain their livelihood, supplementing their income with agricultural produce obtained from rented land. Both of these factors, the pursuit of crafts and commerce and the need for rentable land drew the highland Ethiopian Muslims to the country's towns and made them a more urbanized community than their Christian neighbors. Rentable land was more plentifully available in the vicinity of larger towns because of the holdings of endowed churches.[17] This point is made with particular clarity by V.L. Grottanelli, who stresses the connection of Muslims with rentable church land.[18] I have already indicated that in my view pockets of Muslim inhabitants had become an integral part of the Ethiopian society and were well established before the wars of Ahmad Gran in the sixteenth century.[19]

The declining power of the emperor at Gondar and the political dissension between the local nobility in the late eighteenth century brought about theological controversies in which both the rulers and the people were involved.[20] Both the theological controversies within the Orthodox Church and the general revival of trade in the 1830s helped the spread of Islam.[21] In the 1840s, Muslim merchants of Gondar along with their co-religionists from Adwa, Darita, and Basso spread Islam to areas south of the Blue Nile.[22] Things began to take a different turn in the latter part of the nineteenth century. Christian political power began to revive with Emperor Tewodros (1855–68) and was consolidated by Emperor Yohannis (1871–89). Yohannis proved especially harsh towards Islam, both in the service of his beliefs and as an instrument of political unification. He concentrated his evangelical efforts in Wallo province, whose location between Tigrai in the north, Begemdir and Gojjam to the west, and Shewa to the south separated the core provinces of the empire. Wallo by this time, according to Zewde Gabre-Sellassie, "had become a veritable Islamic state within the heartland of Ethiopia."[23] However true this may have been, it is not a good reason for Yohannis to have disturbed the atmosphere of religious tolerance. In the period of imperial expansion, the formation of a theocratic state was not the best means to preserve Ethiopia's independence, as Zewde Gabre-Sellassie would like us to believe.[24] As a matter of fact, Yohannis's political and religious ideals had no lasting, beneficial effect.

In Bet al-Islam in Gondar, Emperor Yohannis himself razed its mosque in 1881; thereafter he built the Egziabher-Ab church.[25] Muslims of Gondar were offered two choices: either embrace Christianity, or leave the dominions of the emperor.[26] Religious liberty was not restored until the death of Yohannis in 1889 in his wars with Mahdist sudan.[27] Some Muslims of Gondar went to Wallo and to the areas south of the Blue Nile. Those who remained in gondar became more timid and conservative.[28] Emperor Menelik (1889–1913) followed a more tolerant religious policy. Full religious liberty was restored to the now consolidated Ethiopian empire. His era also saw the emergence of a centralized bureaucratic system, which facilitated the expansion of trade. In Gondar, under Gugsa Wale (1910–1932) there was a period of relative peace.[29] Gugsa, a pious man himself, did not interfere in the affairs of the Muslims. Certainly, we have reliable evidence which suggests that for the period between 1900 and 1935 the Gondarine Muslims were not persecuted, but simply ignored. Accordingly, they lived as a submerged group. The government forces affected Bet al-Islam in matters of taxation and administration, and in this way connected it to the surrounding Christian populace.[30]

Of particular importance to the social life of Bet al-Islam was the exercise of the Islamic law, *Shari'a*. The *ulama* (religio-legal establishment) of Gondar administered the *Shari'a* court within the Christian Gondarine administration. The *ulama* did not resort to police power in settling disputes or attempting to control disruptive behavior. Major crimes such as killing or theft were virtually unheard of amongst the Muslims of Gondar. Problems arising from divorce and inheritance cases were referred to the *qadi* (Muslim jurist).[31] Social control in Bet al-Islam was based upon internal sanctions, which were expressed by a strong religious ethic known as *adat* (in Amharic also *adat*, local usage of the *Shari'a* law). *Adat* emanated from the internal self-rule of Bet al-Islam. The public aspects of life reinforced the *Shari'a*.[32] Certainly the *Shari'a* with its concomitant *adat* prevailed over the Christian administration in matters connected with social control.[33] The Christian administration simply collected taxes from craftsmen and merchants.[34]

The *qadis* and *ulama* were financed by contributions from merchants and craftsmen. The Muslim scholars of Bet al-Islam in Gondar received their education in the Qur'anic schools of Wallo province, which by and large had the largest Amharic and Tigrenna speaking Muslim population in the country. Certainly, Wallo was the center of Islamic learning for all the north-western highlands of Ethiopia. In this way it parallelled the role of Harrar, which served as a center of Islamic diffusion to southern and south-western Ethiopia.[35]

The *qadis* and the *ulama* of Gondar, who were educated in the Qur'anic schools of Wallo, were able to translate the Qur'an and the Hadith into Amharic for the general public, *jama'a*. The translation was made every Friday. The process was such that one person read the Arabic version and the other spoke in Amheric so that the *jama'a* could understand the scriptures of the Qur'an and the Hadith.[36] Teachers in the Qur'anic school of Gondar, however, simply taught how to read the Qur'an. This was chiefly because the average Muslim in Gondar could not afford the time or the money to stay in school. Instead, they pursued their profession as merchants and weavers.[37] In the main, the average Muslim in Gondar learned how to read the Qur'an and was, therefore, better educated compared to the average Christian there, who did not learn how to read the Bible.[38] The Qur'an was memorized and recited in the mosque yard of Bet al-Islam. Public prayers were observed and seasonal religious rituals were performed.[39] Muslims of Gondar had lost their external links with other Muslims in other countries[40] and even with Muslims of south-western Ethiopia.[41] This was because the bulk of the export trade from southern and south-western Ethiopia began to be tapped by merchants from Harrar, Wallo, the Gurage lands, and Jimma itself. The activities of the Gondarine merchants in the wider context of south-west Ethiopian trade declined, but their control over the trade of Begemdir and northern Ethiopia continued.[42]

Trade, both local and international, was the main occupation of the Muslims of Gondar. Gondar had rich merchants, who brought commodities from the ports of Matamma and Massawa and distributed them to retail traders. The merchants, who dominated the trade of the wider Red Sea region in which Ethiopia found itself, were mostly Muslims and preferred to deal with their co-religionists at the main points of articulation between Ethiopia and the wider region—Matamma on the Sudan border, west of Gondar; and Massawa on the Red Sea coast in today's Eritrea.[43] Thus, the Ethiopian Muslims happened to master the techniques involved in manipulating long-distance trade and thereby came to preponderate in Gondar's commercial community.[44]

Christian merchants obviously mastered these techniques as well. However, as it has already been noted, Christians had many other opportunities that were basically closed to Muslims, viz, farming, army, church, court, the legal system, etc. The fact that there was a general Christian prejudice against commerce, however, did not stop them in the least from engaging in it when they wanted to.[45] Yet, it is also true that Muslims enjoyed more success when dealing with their co-religionists at Matamma and Massawa.[46] Muslims were the most important elements of the economy of the town throughout the first three-and-a-half decades of the twentieth century. The importation of foreign goods from the coast into the north-western provinces of Begemdir and Gojjam was to a large extent in the hands of the Muslim merchants of Gondar.[47] They played an important part in making the town the center of wholesale trade for much of north-west Ethiopia.[48]

In Gondar itself, much of the trade was conducted by retail traders. These individuals took commodities from the rich merchants of Gondar on the basis of credit and in turn sold the commodities on the basis of credit, either in the weekly Saturday market of Gondar or in the network of local (balagar) markets, which were located within a few hours walk from the town. These traders also travelled within a few hours walk from Gondar to bring the wider regional produce to the town. Thus, they succeeded in bringing iron from Walqayit and wine from Qorata, Yifag, and Darita.[49] Retail merchants and weavers as well used their private houses at Bet al-Islam as stores for their merchandise.[50] Christian customers from the center of town needed to go downhill across the crooked and narrow paths of Bet al-Islam in order to buy whatever foreign commodities they wanted.[51] Weavers worked at home[52] and exchanged their woven cloth for cash and the agricultural produce of the surrounding countryside.[53]

As was the case with most ancient towns of the Ethiopian highlands, Gondar was connected with the port of Massawa. But Gondar's particular advantage was its connection with the Sudan via Matamma. This route connected Gondar with Matamma and Gallabat via Chilga and Wahni. Merchants of Gondar took coffee, gold, civet, honey and wax, hides and skins, butter, ginger, and pepper to Matamma market and exchanged these products for British-made goods. From matamma Sudanese merchants proceeded to Sennar and Khartoum. Merchants of Gondar were never allowed to cross the Amihara river port at Matamma. Thus, they brought home British products like cloth in bales, shawls, corrugated iron sheets, locks, and waterproof canvas cloth used for tents, incense of different kinds, and kerosene.[54] These merchants traded with their own capital and were obviously rich compared to retail traders and weavers.[55]

It is interesting to note that most prosperous merchants of Gondar preferred to trade with Asmara rather than with Matamma. This was because much of the money circulating in Gondar was in their hands. In addition to this, Italian products at Asmara were greater in quantity and lower in price compared to British products at Matamma.[56] The commodities merchants bought at Asmara consisted of cotton and silk cloth of different colors, ornaments, black pepper and other spices, utensils, metal water bottles, knives, sickles, safety pins, needles, and mirrors. Another factor that made Gondar-Asmara trade particularly important was that salt bars (amole) could be brought from Maqelle, a town between Gondar and Asmara.[57] The salt bars were used not only for consumption, but also as a currency. The salt bars continued to serve as the medium of exchange throughout the early period of the twentieth century, but the number of salt bars exchanged for dollar continued to fall.[58] Certainly, Gondar was not the source of long-distance commodities. It simply served as a transit for commodities that came and went through it. But the capital of the Gondarine merchants dominated the trade routes which ran from Gudru to the south of the Blue Nile to Massawa via Gondar.[59]

One important commodity, of internal significance, in which the Muslim merchants of Gondar dealt was cattle. Oral history indicates that the cattle trade, which was formerly a rural activity, became decidedly urban in character in the early part of the twentieth century. The trade in cattle covered long distances and crossed major provincial frontiers. The cattle trade originated in Gudru, south of the Blue Nile. The heyday of cattle droves coincided with the period of relative peace that the twentieth century afforded in contrast with the numerous interruptions and depressions that resulted from the wars of the nineteenth century.[60] The cattle market was generally for internal consumption and exclusively bound to Gondar town. Most of the cattle were consumed by the nobility, at whose tables this luxury good was served.[61] Peasant diets were ordinarily vegetarian. There was also contemporaneous trade in horses that parallelled the cattle trade. The horses originated in jarso, to the south-east in Shewa province and were driven to market in Gondar by way of Bichana in Gojjam.[62] Like cattle, horses were also exclusively bought and owned by the military class.[63]

The trade in cattle fostered the concentration of oxen in the hands of a few well-to-do Muslims. These Muslims rented their oxen to the neighboring Christian peasants who did not have enough cattle or who did not have cattle at all.[64] Lack of statistical material makes it difficult to examine how many Muslims owned oxen. What is certain is that Muslims rented their oxen to farmers of the countryside, and in return received agricultural products during the period of harvest.[65] Much of the agricultural produce was consumed by the large family units as the rich Muslims had the habit of marrying more than one wife.[66] The remainder was distributed to the poor Muslims in Bet al-Islam. But there was no attempt on the part of the rich Muslim merchants to accumulate grain for purposes of trade.[67] As has already been pointed out, Muslims in origin were separated from land, indeed the main means of agricultural production. However, a few sufficiently wealthy Muslims owned oxen, which was another key means of agricultural production.[68]

These merchants also assembled a considerable amount of capital with which they bought commodities and transported them to Asmara. For the most part of the first three-and-a-half decades of the twentieth century, trade from the interior terminated at Asmara. However, some merchants proceeded to Massawa and very occasionally crossed the Red Sea to reach Jidda, where they would receive a better price for their commodities. Such trips were conducted during the *hajj* (pilgrimage).[69] On their return from Jidda pilgrim merchants brought Indian, Persian, and Turkish products such as carpets, silk and cotton cloth, razors, sandals, antimony, etc.[70] This trade to Jidda was one of the ways in which Muslim merchants had an advantage over Christians.

The prosperous merchants, retail traders, and weavers of Gondar did not engage themselves in converting people to Islam during this period. One obvious reason was that they had been persecuted as a result of Emperor Yohannis' anti-Muslim internal policy. Secondly, in the early twentieth century, Gondar itself began to send its young, promising scholars for further Qur'anic education to other centers in Wallo and such Sudanic borderlands as Roseires and Sennar. What mattered for Muslims of Gondar was not so much to spread the Islamic faith as to survive with it, given the fact that they lived amidst the Christian majority.[71]

The conversion to Islam of many believers in traditional religions in the twentieth century was a recurring phenomenon in other parts of Africa, so also in southern Ethiopia.[72] In Gondar itself, the Muslim minority in their enthusiasm for commercial ventures had close and continual contact with government and church officials, who needed them for their commercial importance. Muslim weavers were also needed for their cotton cloth (*shamma*) produce. Yet, the Ethiopian feudal system was hostile to trade and urban life.[73] The system developed the mechanism to segregate Muslims territorially and to ostracize them socially. In response to such a challenge, the Muslim minority became active in commerce and artisanry.[74] What is remarkable about the Muslims of Gondar was that they survived so long and achieved so much in the realm of trade.

Notes

1. I am deeply indebted to my informant countrymen Garima Taffara, Marqani Mohammad and Yussuf Ahmad Tayimu. I hope I have accurately summarized their explanations of the past, which they entrusted me to write. To them, I dedicate this paper with love, affection and pride. I wish to express my warm appreciation and gratitude to my advisor Professor Donald Crummey, who has shared my interest and critically commented on my paper. Suffice it to say, however, that the judgments and interpretations are mine. I am also grateful to Professors Charles Stewart and Ronald Jennings for their careful reading of early drafts of this paper.

2. Taddesse Tamrat, *Church and State in Ethiopia 1270–1527*. London: Oxford University Press, 1972, p. 43.

3. *Ibid. passim.*

4. Edward Ullendorff, *The Ethiopians: An Introduction to Country and People*. London: Oxford University Press, 1973, pp. 69–72.

5. Abraham Demoz, "Moslems and Islam in Ethiopic Literature," *Journal of Ethiopian Studies*, Vol. X, No. 1 (1972), p. 6.

6. Donald Crummey, "Gondarine Rim Land Sales: An Introductory Description and Analysis," *Proceedings of the Fifth International Conference on Ethiopian Studies* (Chicago, n.d.), p. 469.

7. E. Van Donzel, *Foreign Relations of Ethiopia 1642–1700*. Leiden: Brill, 1979, pp. 4–5.

8. *Ibid.*, p. 7. The Yemenites who arrived at Gondar with Hajji Salim saw a completely Muslim village next to the royal court, which was probably Gondar.

9. *Ibid.*, 10.

10. *Ibid.*, See also Merid Wolde Aregay, "Technology in Medieval Ethiopia," unpublished paper presented to the Conference on Ethiopian Feudalism, Chicago 1976, p. 7.

11. Jean Doresse, *Ethiopia*. New York: Putnam, 1959, p. 179.

12. Charles Jacques Poncet, *A Voyage to Ethiopia in the Red Sea and Adjacent Countries*. London: Hakluyt Society, Second Series, 1949.

13. Garima Taffara, an outstanding historian in Gondar, interviewed on 10 September

1979; he was sixty-seven at the time of the interview. Yusuf Ahmad Tayimu, another outstanding historian and a merchant on the Gondar-Matamma and Gondar-Massawa routes. Interviewed on 14 and 15 September 1979. He was sixty-one at the time of the interview.

14. Poncet, p. 61.

15. Ignatius Guidi, *Annales Regum Iyasu Ii et Iyo'as*. Paris, 1910.

16. James Bruce, *Travels to Discover the Source of the Nile*. Edinburgh: G.G.J.J. Robinson, 5 Vols., 1790, Vol. III, p. 198.

17. Garima Taffara and Yussuf Ahmad Tayimu.

18. V. L. Grottanelli, *Missione di Studio al Lago Tana*. Roma: Reali Academeia di Italia, 1938, p. 152. I am indebted to Professor Donald Crummey for drawing my attention to the availability of rentable land in Begemdir province and to the pertinence of Grottanelli's work.

19. Garima Taffara and Yussuf Ahmad Tayimu. See also M. Abir, *Ethiopia: The Era of the Princes: The Challenge of Islam and the Re-unification of the Christian Empire*. New York: Praeger, 1968, p. 71.

20. Abir, *The Era of the Princes*, pp. 39–40.

21. M. Abir, "Trade and Politics in the Ethiopian Region 1830–1855," unpublished Ph.D. dissertation, London, 1964, *passim*.

22. "The Emergence and Consolidation of the Monarchies of Enarea and Jima in the first Half of the Nineteenth Century," *Journal of African History*, Vol. VI, 2 (1965), p. 207.

23. Zewde Gabre-Sellassie, *Yohannes IV of Ethiopia: A Political Biography*. Oxford: At the Clarendon Press, 1975, p. 100.

24. *Ibid.*, p. 257.

25. Garima Taffara. See also Gabira Madihin Kidane, "Yohannis IV: Religious Aspects of His Internal Policy," unpublished B.A. thesis, Addis Ababa University, May 1972, p. 25.

26. R. A. Caulk, "Religion and the State in Nineteenth Century Ethiopia," in *Journal of Ethiopian Studies*, Vol. X, No. 1 (1972), p. 28.

27. Garima Taffara. See also Doresse, *Ethiopia*, p. 202.

28. Garima Taffara and Yussuf Ahmad Tayimu.

29. Garima Tafarra and Yussuf Ahmad Tayimu. However, Gugsa's period also saw the

emergence of local bandits in the western border of Begemder. Generally, the social atmosphere in central border of Begemder was not disturbed. Gondar town was completely peaceful and trade continued unhampered by bandits on the way to Matamma. All the bandits asked of merchants was a modest amount of money which they willingly paid.

30. Garima Taffara and yussuf Ahmad Tayimu.
31. *Ibid.*
32. *Ibid.*
33. *Ibid.*
34. *Ibid.*
35. *Ibid.*
36. Yussuf Ahmad Tayimu and Marqani Mohammad. The latter was a well known merchant in Gondar who traded on the Gondar-Asmara and Gondar-Matamma routes. Interviewed on 12 September 1979. He was seventy-four at the time of the interview.
37. *Ibid.* Grottanelli, p. 159.
38. Garima Taffara and Yussuf Ahmad Tayimu.
39. Marqani Mohammad and Yussuf Ahmad Tayimu.
40. Grottanelli, *Missione,* Rome, p. 60.
41. Marqani Mohammad and Yussuf Ahman Tayimu.
42. *Ibid.*
43. *Ibid.* See also M. Abir, "Trade and Politics in the Ethiopian Region, 1830–1855," p. 17.
44. Garima Taffara and Yussuf Ahmad Tayimu. See also Abir, *passim.*
45. Garima Taffara and Yussuf Ahmad Tayimu.
46. *Ibid.*
47. *Ibid.*
48. *Ibid.*
49. *Ibid.*
50. *Ibid.* Marqani Mohammad.
51. Marqani Mohammad and Yussuf Ahmad Tayimu.
52. Grottanelli, *Missione,* p. 160.
53. Marqani Mohammad and Yussuf Ahmad Tayimu.

54. *Ibid.*

55. *Ibid.*

56. *Ibid.*

57. *Ibid.*

58. *Ibid.*

59. Garima Taffara and Yussuf Ahmad Tayimu.

60. Garima Taffara.

61. *Ibid.*

62. Marqani Mohammad.

63. Garima Taffara.

64. Marqani Mohammad and Yussuf Ahmad Tayimu.

65. *Ibid.*

66. *Ibid.*

67. *Ibid.*

68. *Ibid.* and Garima Taffara.

69. *Ibid.*

70. *Ibid.*

71. *Ibid.*

72. For a cogent analysis of the spread of Islam in southern Ethiopia in the twentieth century, see Edward Ullendorff's essay on the Hbasha in b. Lewis, Ch. Pellat and J. Schact, *The Encyclopedia of Islam*. Leiden: Brill, Vol. III. London: 1965.

73. Merid Wolde Aregay, "Technology," p. 5.

74. Grotannelli, *Missione*, p. 159.

CHAPTER SIX

Dar Sila,

The Sultanate in Precolonial Times,

1870–1916[1]

LIDWIEN KAPTEIJNS

F OR THE SULTANATE OF DAR SILA, as for the other sultanates of the Chado-Sudanese frontier, the French conquest of Wadai in 1909 sounded the death-knell over its existence as a small independent Sudanic state. However, when Sultan Bakhit Abu Risha of Dar Sila sent a letter of submission to Fort Lamy, neither he nor the French realized that the social and political institutions typical of a Sudanic state were incompatible with its incorporation into the French Empire and the European-dominated world economy.

In the years following 1909, therefore, each party tried to work out some form of peaceful coexistence acceptable to both. Dar Sila expected the French Government to behave like its former overlords, the sultanates of Dar Fur and of Wadai. Although the French were at this stage ready to limit their demands, they expected Dar Sila not only to recognize French suzerainty, but also to be responsive to some of their ideals of progress, notably the abolition of the slave trade, the promotion of "legitimate" trade, a uniform system of taxation (in cash), and peaceful relations with neighboring states. Since each party expected the other to act according to its own political (and economic) code, misunderstanding and distrust marred mutual relations from the beginning. From the diplomatic correspondence and administrative reports of the period it is evident that each party frantically tried to understand the other and to make itself understood, moreover, that both failed to do so and hence often misjudged the other's intentions. The French reconquest of Dar Sila in 1916, which led to the deposition and exile of the sultan and to the reorganization of the state, may well have been a result of this basic misunderstanding.

This chapter is primarily concerned with the political history of Dar Sila and—as far as the sources allow—with the political and social organization of the precolonial state. While it analyzes the revolutionary impact of the beginnings of French colonial rule, it stops short of a discussion of the colonial period as a whole. It bases itself on administrative reports preserved in the French and British colonial archives, the Arabic archives of the Mahdist state, the Arabic correspondence of the sultans of Dar Sila and, to some extent, on oral sources collected by the author on the Sudanese side of the Chado-Sudanese border, in Dar Fur, Dar Masalit, and Dar Sinyar.

Dar Sila was the southernmost state of a chain of sultanates that formed the border between the historical sultanate of Dar Fur (in western Sudan) and that of Wadai (in eastern Chad). In contrast to the sultanates to its north, Dar Sila had an abundant rainfall (600–800 milligrams per year), and hence a rich vegetation and wildlife. Its main crops were sorghum, millet, and cotton; its pastures sustained livestock of many types (but no camels). The bulk of its population was formed by the Daju, who gave the sultanate its alternative name of "Dar Daju," of "the land of the Daju." However, Dar Daju was also inhabited by a large number of nomadic peoples (the Salamat, Terjam, Haymat, Missiriyya, Bani Halba, and others) and by people of more southern extraction such as the Kara, Gula, and Banda, many of whom had been brought to Dar Sila as slaves. Dar Sila's northeastern border was inhabited by the Sinyar and by groups of Fur and Masalit whose tribal homelands lay further to the east.

The historical core of the sultanate was formed by the Daju, who were bound together by linguistic, historical, religious, economic, and political ties. Being Daju meant first of all that a person spoke the Daju language, which belongs to the Nilo-Saharan family of languages and is at present spoken by approximately 50,000 people, 300,000 of whom live in Chad.[2] A second element of Daju identity was the belief in a common descent and a shared history.

When the French came upon the scene in 1909, the Daju had (and further developed) an elaborate tradition of origin. That the Daju originally inhabited Dar Fur—where memories of Daju Empire, subsequently replaced by that of the Tunjur, have been preserved—is commonly accepted. The Daju place their migration to Dar Sila at the beginning of the eighteenth century, but their oral traditions cannot be verified beyond the reign of Sultan Anqarib (ca. 1813–1851) or that of his son Muhammad Bulad (1851–1879).[3] A third element of Daju identity was a common religion. Today the Daju royal family claims descent from the family of the Prophet, but when the Daju came to Dar Sila they were probably still unaffected by Islam. In most parts of the Wadai-Dar Fur region the beginnings of Islamization are associated with the foundation of the sultanates of Wadai and Dar Fur in the first half of the seventeenth century. Even then Islam remained for many years the religion of the court and the ruling elite, while the subjects were Muslims only in the sense that they were subject to a Muslim ruler and hence not enslavable. On both levels of society, that of the rulers and that of the subjects, customs and beliefs of pre-Islamic origin continued to exist until the colonial period. For example, consultation by the rulers with the "oracle of the termite-hill," to predict the future from the movements of the ants and a harvest feast held to appease the spirit of the grain seem to have been typically Daju customs, and the belief in spirits that populated trees or water holes and in rainmaking rituals were common coin in the Wadai-Dar Fur region as a whole.[4]

The Daju also shared a common mode of subsistence. They were farmers, and most of the land of Dar Sila was Daju land, that is to say, belonging to

Daju clans and sub-clans, represented by their *maliks* (chiefs). Even if the Daju were not the state's richest subjects, they were the most stable inhabitants and hence more liable to regular taxation, administration of justice, and demands of military service than was true of the various nomadic peoples of the country. Farmers and nomads together formed the class of the free subjects or commoners (*masakin*) of the sultanate. Below them were the slaves, above them the ruling class. The former consisted of *Fertit* and *Kirdi*, generic names for the non-Muslim (and hence enslavable) peoples who originated in the southern marches of the Dar Fur and Wadai sultanates. Slaves were owned by both commoners and rulers, but the latter owned many more. Domestic slaves seem to have enjoyed a status that was one notch below that of their masters and could hence be higher than that of a commoner. However, since slaves were a major export article in Dar Sila, there were many trade slaves who were not incorporated into the social structure on a permanent basis; they formed a distinct class ranked below that of the commoners. Intermediate in status between the domestic and trade slaves were those slaves belonging to the nobility who were settled in special villages. These slaves were set apart from, and socially inferior to the free subjects of the realm.[5]

The government or ruling class was predominately Daju, another factor that gave the Daju an identity of their own. In Dar Sila, as in the other sultanates of the area, the position of sultan was hereditary in the male line. However, although being a sultan's son was a prerequisite to ascending to the throne, it was not necessary to be the son of the last reigning sultan. The death of a monarch, therefore, usually caused a fierce succession dispute (and sometimes civil war) between the sons, brothers, and paternal uncles of the deceased, each of whom had an entourage of armed cavaliers, consisting of close male relatives, selected commoners, and military slaves. The reigning monarch often tried to predetermine the succession during his lifetime by appointing one of his relatives as his successor, and by allowing him to maintain a larger number of retainers than the other members of the ruling elite.

Since the entourages of the various princes and dignitaries—best compared to modern political parties—vied for power not only with each other but also with the sultan himself, the latter safeguarded his position by maintaining more footsoldiers and horsemen than all other dignitaries combined, and by appointing slaves to important military and administrative positions. In 1911, for example, Sultan Bakhit Abu Risha had an army of 1,000 men, of whom 400 were horsemen. His son and heir apparent, Dhahab, had 300 men, including 100 horsemen, while the other major dignitaries, of whom two were slaves and at least three Daju princes, had together 350 footmen and 100 mounted retainers.[6] In spite of the infighting within the ranks of the royal family, the solidarity of the royal clan of Dar Sila (and the other small frontier sultanates) was stronger than that of the larger states of Wadai and Dar Fur. While possible pretenders to the throne were blinded (and hence forever disqualified from becoming sultan) in Wadai—and were pensioned off into obscurity in Dar Fur—in Dar Sila, Dar Masalit, Dar Qimr, and Dar Tama they gathered around the sultan and became the pillars of the central government.

In July 1911 a French official in Dar Sila wrote:

The only political organization that exists is the will of the sultan, surrounded by his brothers, his sons, and numerous officials.[7]

This observation does not do full justice to Dar Sila's government. It is true that the king disposed of life and death and was accountable to no one but God. However, the will of the sultan was strictly circumscribed by custom. The king could violate custom, for example by raising taxes, but only at the risk of causing general discontent or even popular revolt. Dar Sila had moreover a hierarchy of titled and untitled officials and a system of administration that operated on the same principles as the other states of the Wadai-Dar Fur region.[8] By this system the country was divided into larger and smaller districts (administrative and private estates), which were ruled by representatives of the central government. According to Berre, the Daju sultanate consisted of four until the reign of Abu Risha (1879–1900), who doubled their number, and put four officials called *kamkolaks* in charge of the interior and four officials called *maqdums* in charge of the frontier provinces. The reality, however, was more complex; close relatives and favorites of the king ruled—virtually as sultans—areas that might be larger or smaller than the jurisdictions of the officials mentioned by Berre.[9]

The French official quoted above was right, however, in pointing out that the most important and remunerative offices were occupied by the uncles, brothers, sons and cousins of the sultan. They discharged their administrative duties from Goz Beida, where their presence was required as councilors of the king. To provide his councilors with a livelihood the sultan granted them lands and villages, whose *maliks* (chiefs) and inhabitants were under their jurisdiction, and whose production was taxed by them for their own benefit. Since the sultan provided in the same way for dependent (female) relatives who did not have an administrative function, the area around the capital was divided up into small estates, whose owners owed the sultan few, if any, taxes. In the outlying areas the administrative units were larger, but there too a central government representative (often a royal relative or military slave) was imposed upon the local *maliks* and nomadic *sheikhs*, and there too villages belonging to some notable or other formed islands of immunity or small private estates.[10] In the larger districts a central government agent was expected to collect taxes (the yield of which was divided between the local chiefs, himself, and the sultan), to supervise the administration of justice by the local chief, to guard the borders and, in case of war, to raise a general levy.

The commoners, Daju and non-Daju alike, owed the state a part of what they produced and some labor services. These dues, which were similar to those levied on the commoners in other sultanates of the area, included the Islamic taxes of *zakah* and *fitra* (both grain taxes), a tax on livestock (also called *zakah*), and irregular levies of honey, ghee, and homespun cotton cloth. The sultan had moreover a right to all runaway slaves and livestock (the *hamil*), and to a half of the ivory procured within the state's boundaries.[11] The production of the slaves owned by commoners was taxed as part of that of their masters. However, the largest number of slaves was owned by the ruling class and—if they did not serve as armed retainers, concubines, or domestic servants—lived in slave villages. It is probable that these slaves had a larger part of their production appropriated than the commoners had. In addition, their offspring were freely disposed of by their masters.[12]

The government left much of the grain and livestock it collected as taxes on the spot, sending for part of it only when the need arose, for example, to celebrate the Islamic festivals, to entertain travellers and royal refugees, or to reward dependents, holy men, and other favorites. In times of war the local grainstores were opened to the soldiers; in times of drought—and to a lesser extent in any year—the public grain was distributed to the needy.[13]

Aside from conspicuous consumption and redistribution, trade was a third use to which the income from taxes was directed. Imported goods—cloth, clothes, other articles of personal adornment, horse furniture, exotic table luxuries such as tea, coffee, and sugar, carpets, crockery, gilded swords, and rifles—were the badge of noble status and their possession a prerogative by which the rulers distinguished themselves from the commoners.[14] Since the road from Dar Sila to the Mediterranean trade centers was long and arduous, and transport primitive, exports had to be either of small bulk and high value (like ivory, ostrich feathers, skins, spices, rhinoceros-horn), or able to take care of their own transport (like cattle and slaves). Ivory and slaves were Dar Sila's major exports. Since the extent to which these could be extracted from the subjects was limited, the government regularly sent hunting and slave-raiding expeditions to the south[15] Thus it procured the products that could pay for the imports brought to Goz Beida by the long-distance traders: the Fezzan, *jallaba* traders, and West Africans. The long-distance trade was regulated by the sultan, who controlled the movements and activities of the traders. It therefore served to perpetuate the privileged position of the ruling class.

The description of the organization of the Daju state presented above is, in broad outline, valid for the whole period between 1870–1909. While the nature of the available sources does not allow for a reconstruction of the development of the political and social institutions of precolonial Dar Sila, it is possible to present a more dynamic picture of the eventful political history of the sultanate.

The Age of Expansion

Wedged in between the larger sultanates of Wadai and Dar Fur, Dar Sila's independence was always precarious. Although the Daju claimed to have migrated to Dar Sila to rid themselves of the Fur yoke, the Fur sultans looked upon the sultanate as a tributary state. As late as 1912, the sultan of Dar Fur wrote to Sultan Bakhit of Dar Sila:

> Undoubtedly you witnessed the earlier days as they were, and it must be known to you that your ancestors and father were subject to the government of Dar Fur, maintaining good relations with it and living with the approval of its rulers in pleasant association with one another.[16]

The Daju sultan politely denied the Fur claim by defining their relationship in different and more egalitarian terms:

> We and you are today neighbors in God, and neighborliness is sacred. Between us is the book of God, and the Book is sacred. We are related by marriage, and relationship by marriage is sacred. [Moreover] we are sultans, and being a sultan is sacred.[17]

In statements to the British and French colonial governments the Daju sultan denied the Fur claims more explicitly:

> I am informing your noble government so that you may fully understand that we have been an independent sultanate from the olden days. Until today no power has entered our country and—praised be the Lord and His Prophet—until the present we have remained in this state.
>   As long as we have been in this, our country, we have not paid

taxes to the Fur.[18]

Whether one regards Bakhit's statements as truth or falsehood depends on one's interpretation of the terms "independent" (*sultanah qa'imah bi nafsiha*) and "taxes" (*al-miri*). In the Wadai-Dar Fur region, as elsewhere in the world, some states were more independent than others, and while Dar Sila may have regarded the *diwan* or tribute it paid—now to Dar Fur, then to Wadai—as presents to rulers of equal status, the larger sultanates regarded it as a symbol of submission. The travel accounts of both al-Tunisi (in ca. 1810) and Nachtigal (in 1874) refer to Dar Sila as an autonomous state that paid tribute to both big neighbors in turn, or even at the same time. There is no doubt, however, that Dar Sila was a separate state and a sultanate in its own right.[19]

This situation prevailed until the 1870s, which witnessed a drastic change in the balance of powers in the area. In 1874 the Dar Fur Sultanate was conquered from the south by the slave troops of the merchant-king al-Zubayr Rahma and subsequently incorporated into the Turco-Egyptian (Turkish) Sudan. The Turkish regime, which had been established in the Nile Valley as early as 1821, lasted only nine years in the western Sudan. In that period it succeeded in killing a number of Fur princes and sultans-in-exile, and in alienating the people of the area by its ruthless taxation policy and plunderings. The rulers of the western frontier—the sultans of Dar Qimr and Dar Tama, and the chiefs of the Jabal, Erenga, Masalit and Zaghawa—offered their submission and had to allow the establishment of a number of Turkish camps, from where Turkish troops collected taxes, amicably or forcibly. Alarmed by the rumors about the Turkish firearms, the sultans of Wadai and Dar Sila anxiously watched their eastern borders. Since the Turkish troops never penetrated further than eastern Dar Tama, armed clashes with the sultanate of Wadai were avoided. The Daju, however, acting upon the principle that the best defense is a good offense, decided to come to the aid of their eastern neighbors, the Sinyar, and inflicted a number of (inconclusive) defeats upon Turkish garrisons in the area. It was in these campaigns that the future sultan Ishaq Abu Risha, nicknamed "the yellow bull," earned his spurs.[20]

The outbreak of the Mahdiyya, the millenarian movement that declared the holy war against the Turkish conquerors in 1882, meant the end of the Turkish regime in the Sudan. Although Khartoum, the capital, was not liberated until 1885, the surrender of Slatin Pasha in December 1883 marked the end of the Turkiyya in Dar Fur. The sultans of the west, including those of Wadai and Dar Sila, sent letters of allegiance to the Mahdi. As long as this paper allegiance was all that was required, relations between the sultans and the Mahdist state remained good. However, when the centralizing policy of the Mahdi's successor (1885–1898) began to have its impact upon the west, the western sultanates closed their ranks against the Mahdist state and staged "the revolt of Abu Jummayza" (1888–1889).

This revolt, which began as a popular revolt against the misbehavior of the Mahdist troops in the area, owed its name to a local *faqih* or holy man, Abu Jummayza. The latter became the charismatic leader of the revolt not only as the spokesman of the harried masses, but also as the figurehead around whom the sultans of the area could gather without having to subordinate themselves to each other. Under Abu Jummayza's symbolic leadership the sultans set out to restore the status quo of before 1874, that is to say, among other things, to restore the Fur Sultanate to the Fur sultan-in-exile, Abu'l-Khayrat. Among the eight sultans who were on Abu Jummayza's side was the Daju Sultan Ishaq Abu Risha (1879–1900), who sent out an army under the leadership of his son, the future sultan Bakhit. The western revolt caused panic in the Mahdist ranks and for a moment jeopardized the Mahdist administration of Dar Fur.

However, the western armies—no match for the firearms of the Mahdists, demoralized by the death (from smallpox) of their leader and divided as a result of the jealousies between the sultans—were defeated in battle in February 1889. The different ethnic contingents dispersed; Abu'l-Khayrat fled to Dar Sila. Although the Mahdist governor reported Bakhit Abu Risha among the casualties, Bakhit returned to Dar Sila unharmed and lived to succeed his father in 1900. The westerners paid dearly for their revolt when a punitive expedition plundered the area already stricken by drought. Only Dar Sila and Wadai, whose borders the Mahdist troops were not allowed to cross, escaped punishment.[21]

In spite of its military victories the Mahdist state never succeeded in completely subduing the western sultanates, let alone rule them. The power vacuum that had come into being at the fall of the Dar Fur sultanate and that neither Turks nor Mahdists had been able to fill, offered opportunities for political aggrandizement to the sultans of Wadai and Dar Sila.

When Dar Fur was conquered in 1874, the sultanate fell into its constituent parts, mainly ethnic groups, none of which was a match either to Dar Fur's old rival, Wadai, or to its successors, the Turkish and Mahdist regimes. Alienated by both Turks and Mahdists, the rulers of Dar Fur's western border turned to Wadai for protection. Wadai welcomed the opportunity to extend its sphere of influence and to create a series of buffer states along its eastern border. On condition that the small states recognized its overlordship and paid a small tribute, Wadai was ready to restrain its own ambitions in the area, to allow independence in domestic affairs, to act as arbiter in interstate and intertribal disputes, and to offer support against outside threats.

The Mahdiyya was one such threat, and the Mahdist administration was well aware of the role that Wadai played in the affairs of the western frontier. The *Borqawi*, as the sultan of Wadai was called in the Mahdist correspondence, was denounced for inciting the westerners to rebellion, for supplying them with men and arms, and for following a policy of territorial expansion:

> He [the sultan of Wadai] has been tempted into something which could not be held against him before, nor against his ancestors who have been at the head of the Borqu: taking possession of the western districts which are an integral part of Dar Fur.[22]

Like Wadai, Dar Sila attempted to expand eastward into the troubled provinces of the old Dar Fur sultanate. When the Dar Furstate began to totter, Sultan Muhammad Bulad (1850–1879) first conquered Dar Fongoro in the southeast, and subsequently annexed Dar Galfige and Dar Sinyar, which had all been integral parts of Dar Fur.[23] During the Mahdiyya, when Sultan Abu Risha occupied the Daju throne, Dar Sila tried to bring the whole area southwest of Jabal Marra into its sphere of influence. Two (undated) letters that Abu Risha wrote to the local chiefs of the area leave no doubt about his political ambitions:

> Know that you were formerly subject to the people of the east, but subsequently I have taken possession of my whole *dar*.
> We inform you that my son 'Ulla is coming to you with my letter. Don't ever trouble him, for he is the go-between me and you.
> You know, my sons, that this is how it goes in this world; formerly you had your own sultan, that of Dar Fur, but now things have fallen apart and you have become kingless, like goats without a shepherd. Everybody is raiding you, the Masalat, the nomads, and our people as well. Now I have chosen you for myself; you have the *aman* (promise of security) of God, the Prophet, and myself. No one will interfere with you, and if anyone attacks you, you must let me know, for I can deal with him.
> However, on the arrival of my messengers, you who are mentioned in the letter, and all the people of the districts close to you who are with you, summon everybody and read my letter. All of you without exception must rise and come to me, together and without delay, if you want peace and quiet. By God's will you will find tranquillity. If you refuse to come to me and disobey my present order, my sons, don't blame me but blame yourselves. Beware of disobedience and stubbornness. Greetings in conclusion.[24]

The period between 1874–1898, therefore, which was a Time of Troubles for the other frontier states, was for Dar Sila an age of expansion. Not only did it increase its territory as a result of its conquests and annexations, but also its population. Many slaves from the south were settled in villages along the Bahr Azum and elsewhere; many refugees from Dar Fur—sometimes complete tribes—were given a habitat along the eastern border and in and around Goz Beida and Kafiakingi. Aside from the pilgrims, many foreign traders came to Goz Beida attracted by the large supply and low price of slaves.[25]

Emboldened by its success, Dar Sila even tried to shake off the political and economic yoke of Wadai. Two incidents recorded in the Mahdist correspondence and preserved in oral tradition illustrate this. In the 1880s the Daju Sultan tried to open up a trade route to North Africa that would bypass Wadai; in 1891 Abu Risha defied his Wadaian overlord by refusing to give up the booty that he had captured from the Fur, and to which the king of Wadai claimed a right. Both attempts failed. Chastised by the Wadaian army Abu Risha realized that he, just like the other frontier states, had to recognize Wadai's suzerainty. In 1896, after the Daju war with the new sultanate of Dar Masalit, he promptly obeyed orders from Wadai to release his distinguished war captive, the queen-mother of the Masalit.[26] In general, however, Wadai and Dar Sila operated hand-in-glove in this period. Dar Sila's relations with its other (former) overlords, the Fur sultans-in-exile, were in contrast often strained.

What passed between the Daju Sultan and Harun, the Fur "shadow-sultan" during the Turkiyya (1874–1879), is not known. Harun came to the borders of Dar Sila before fleeing to Dar Qimr, where he was finally overtaken by the Turks and killed. Was Harun refused refuge in Dar Sila or did he himself prefer to turn away from safety and to go north? Harun's successor, 'Abd Allah Dud Banga (1879–1884) disputed Abu Risha's conquest of Dar Sinyar and Dar Galfige. Hotly pursued by the Mahdist army, Dud Banga had nothing but words to fight with and soon fled to Omdurman, where he was kept a hostage.[27] A later "shadow-sultan," Abu'l-Khayrat Ibrahim (1889–1891), was initially on good terms with Dar Sila. He took refuge with the Daju at least twice, once before and once. after the revolt of Abu Jummayza by which he hoped to recover his throne. He was given a sizable plot of land and received a Daju princess in marriage, but in the end he fell afoul of Abu Risha, was defeated in the battle of Korlali and driven back to Dar Fur. The incident was described by Bakhit Abu Risha in a letter to the French:

In the time of Abu Risha, Abu'l-Khayrat, sultan of Fur, was expelled by Janu and took refuge with us. We intervened between him and Janu, and Janu ran away and fled from fighting us. We treated Abu'l-

Khayrat generously, as our Prophet Muhammad told us. . . .

We treated him perfectly well; but he was nevertheless out to destroy us and to take up abode in our country. He assembled his armies from among the Fur, the [Ma]salat, the Runga, and all the nomad tribes: the Bani Halba, the Faratim, the Terjam, and the Salamat, living in their midst. They contended with us in battle. My father, sultan Abu Risha, sent me out to fight them. I came upon them in Korali, on a Friday morning. When the [two] groups met and the parties clashed, and many were killed on both sides, Abu'l-Khayrat and his party fled and ran away to their country.[28]

Soon afterwards, in 1891, Abu'l-Khayrat was killed, according to some, by the hand of his distant cousin and successor, 'Ali Dinar. The latter, deserted by most of his adherents, decided to throw in his lot with the Mahdist state rather than with Wadai and the western front. This was particularly unpopular with the Masalit and the Daju, at whose hands he suffered a similar fate to that of Abu'l-Khayrat:

The same [occurred] with 'Ali Dinar. He even left his horse behind and fled walking on foot. We took from them 100 rifles, seven kettledrums, a number of women with their children, even the knife on his forearm, even the teakettle and teacups, his crockery and all that he possessed. They escaped with nothing but their lives.[29]

Whether 'Ali Dinar was despoiled because he had decided to join the Mahdiyya, or whether he joined the Mahdiyya because he was despoiled of all he had, cannot be known with certainty. What is certain, however, is that the former Fur overlords made unreliable protégés, and that the former vassal, Dar Sila, with its "Drang nach Osten" into Fur territory, was a capricious and imperious protector.

The Advent of Colonial Rule

The year 1898, like 1874, marked a watershed in the history of the Wadai-Dar Fur region. In that year, the British "reconquest" of the Nile Valley put an end to the Mahdist state and ushered in a new colonial period. The government of Dar Fur was taken over by the Fur prince and "shadow-sultan," 'Ali Dinar (1898–1916), whom the Anglo-Egyptian Government recognized as an autonomous ruler paying a nominal tribute. The same year witnessed the death of Sultan Yusuf of Wadai (1874–1898), which plunged Wadai into civil war. Muhammad Salih Dud Murra (1902–1909), who emerged victorious from this war, was soon preoccupied with the French advance upon his western border.

When Sultan Bakhit Abu Risha succeeded his father to the throne of Dar Sila in 1900, therefore, the international situation had drastically changed and was in flux. The restored Dar Fur sultanate on his eastern border put an end to Dar Sila's eastward expansion and formed a threat—admittedly distant and as yet mainly ideological—to its independence. In the north, Bakhit had to keep a close watch over the civil war in Wadai in order to be able to lend support to whichever pretender would win the throne and to make the best of any opportunity that would allow him to loosen the ties of dependence. Dar Sila was not in direct danger from the British (who had conquered the Nile Valley), nor from the French (who did not conquer Wadai until 1909), but both powers were already forces to be reckoned with, if only to wield against Dar Sila's imperious neighbors, Dar Fur and Wadai.

In spite of the fact that the Daju, before 'Ali Dinar's return to Dar Fur, had supported another Fur pretender, one who had subsequently been deposed by 'Ali, relations between the new Fur Sultan and Dar Sila were initially good. 'Ali Dinar wrote to Abu Risha to thank him for ruling south-western Dar Fur during the Times of Trouble, and to announce that he would now take over the administration of the area himself. The two agreed upon their common border, which seems to have left Dar Sinyar and Dar Fongoro in Dar Sila.[30] 'Ali Dinar moreover received a daughter of Abu Risha, Fatima Amm Raqiq, in marriage to seal the pact,[31] and the fact that he accepted the position of son-in-law, which traditionally gave many obligations and very few rights, may have reassured Abu Risha. However, 'Ali Dinar's humility seems to have been just a tactic to gain time. Once he had secured his throne, and after he had defeated the upstart sultan of the Masalit in battle (in 1905), he changed his policy in word and deed. In his letters he began to stress that Dar Sila was historically a Fur dependency and that its sultan should therefore look to al-Fashir for guidance. His deeds were even more offensive, particularly when he began to harass parties of traders and pilgrims coming from Dar Sila, even when these parties included Bakhit's own sons and were heading for the holy places. Bakhit, who saw Dar Sila's communications with the outside world threatened, wrote to the British stating his country's independence in unambiguous terms and requesting the British to remove 'Ali Dinar's roadblocks from the trade routes leading through southern Dar Fur and the Bahr al-Ghazal.[32] However, from 1909 onwards, Bakhit's hopes and fears came to focus upon the French, who conquered Wadai in June of that year.

There are two indications that Dar Sila tried to take advantage of the French invasion to loosen its ties with Wadai. Just before the conquest of Abesher it encroached upon Wadai's monopoly over the ivory of Dar Kibet, which so angered Sultan Dud Murra that the two countries were on the verge of war when the French moved in. Moreover, rather than tying his fate to that of Wadai, the Daju Sultan bypassed Abesher and sent a letter of submission directly to Fort Lamy. He did this before he paid allegiance to the new puppet king of Wadai (Adam Asil) and before the first French lieutenant had visited Goz Beida.[33] The French, however, treated Dar Sila as a dependency of Wadai, and this may have contributed to Dar Sila's change of heart about them, which threw the second French expedition visiting Goz Beida into such panic that they called for immediate reinforcements from Abesher. The treaty Bakhit was forced to sign however, was a treaty with the French:

From the Commander of the Faithful, Sultan Muhammad Bakhit, son of Sultan Ishaq Abu Risha. The reason for this document comes from the French: Between us and them peace (*aman*), a treaty and covenant have been concluded. There will be no war between us and them ever. All this [has been agreed upon] with Governor Captain (*Qabitayn*), the *wazir* of France.

The condition or conditions which exist between us and them are: To refrain from war with the tribes, except with the one that attacks us, and [even then] with their [French] permission. To rule justly as God—elevated is He—has ordained; we will abstain from deceit. The French will be the protectors and we the rulers in our country. The roads will be open for the traders and for all the commoners. Slaves will not be sold anymore. We will keep the firearms in our own possession except when they are needed to kill a thief or aggressor. Whenever we are harmed by neighbors, we will not attack them unless with their [French] permission. Whenever [the] Captain wants to count the people, he has my permission to do so.[34]

The treaty did not mention the tax Dar Sila was to pay. It was fixed in money (5000 *riyal* or 15,000 francs per year), but was paid mainly in livestock and sometimes in grain and ivory.

Bakhit, who acted upon the understanding that he would rule a virtually independent Dar Sila under the protection of a strong but distant overlord, can hardly have welcomed the treaty. Its terms, however, which neither he nor the French expected to see enforced immediately, threw less doubt upon his policy towards the French than did the latter's defeat in battle at the hands of the Masalit in January 1910. Distressed that he might have been betting on the wrong horse, Bakhit approached the sultan of the Masalit, assuring him of Daju support in future actions against the French. At the same time he wrote an angry letter to the puppet sultan of Wadai, whom he reproached for having dissuaded him from attacking the French detachment in Goz Beida in November 1909.[35] Neither Bakhit nor the other frontier sultans, however, attempted a rapprochement with Sultan 'Ali Dinar, whose irreconcilable attitude towards the French made him a natural ally. Apparently they feared and mistrusted the ambitious sultan of Dar Fur as much as they did the French. The French soon recovered from their unexpected and unnecessary defeat. In 1910 and 1911 they won a number of battles in Dar Masalit, held a number of punitive expeditions, and suppressed a serious revolt in eastern Wadai. In 1912 all effective resistance against the imposition of their rule came to an end.

While submission to the French delivered the frontier states from the violence of the French armies, it opened the door to a host of unfamiliar and burdensome demands. In the short run the hardships caused by French demands were overshadowed by the consequences of the wrath of 'Ali Dinar, who used military and economic weapons to punish the sultanates for deserting what he regarded as his cause. However, in contrast to the small states to its north—the Masalit, Qimr and Tama—Dar Sila kept largely out of harm's way. The French, afraid that Dar Sila might become another Dar Masalit, treated it with kid gloves, contenting themselves with regular protestations of loyalty and a partial payment of the imposed tax.[36] Only in 1912, when Goz Beida received a French garrison with a resident French captain, did French rule come to weigh more heavily upon the Daju. As for the Fur, Dar Sila was distant enough to be spared the violence of 'Ali Dinar's armies. Even the boycott of the long-distance trade with North Africa, engineered by 'Ali Dinar and the Sanusi sheikh in the Libyan desert, had little effect in Dar Sila and, if anything, increased the volume of trade along Dar Sila's trade route to the east, which led through the British Bahr al-Ghazal. In the years following 1912, Dar Sila's relations with Dar Fur gradually improved, reaching a climax in 1916, just before both sultans were driven from their capitals, by the British troops in the case of 'Ali Dinar, and by the French troops in the case of Bakhit.[37]

After the advent of the French garrison in Goz Beida (and in reaction to it), a strong anti-French faction arose, which pressed for war with the French and had strong pro-Fur sympathies. This war party, led by Bakhit's son, Dhahab, whipped up so much Daju sentiment against the "infidel" invaders that on several occasions it came very close to leading a general attack of Daju tribesmen against them. On at least one such occasion Fur involvement was evident, when a trading mission from Dar Fur showed up with a surprising number of slave attendants, all armed to the teeth.[38] Sultan Bakhit was wavering. In his letters to the French he denied any association with 'Ali Dinar in either past or present and protested his loyalty to the French:

> If you ask about 'Ali Dinar, his father did not have the status of sultan; but as for myself, from Sultan Bokdoru the title of sultan has come down in a continuous line from X to Y to Sultan Bakhit. In view of this, how can I—one of the sons of sultans who have succeeded each other in one continuous line—how can I be subject to the son of a commoner?
>
> I will not betray the French, for I asked you, wrote to you and dealt with you before you asked, wrote to and made a covenant with me. This [betrayal] would not be right and does not root itself in the mind of a wise man; it points at the false claims of oppressors who allege that I am conspiring with 'Ali Dinar. The Fur and I have been neighbors, and a great battle has taken place between us so that on our side men were killed and on their side many more. We took all their weapons—you have seen the weapons with your [own] eyes—and left them neither woman nor horse nor anything, so that 'Ali Dinar fled on foot.
>
> How can we, in view of this hostility, join forces with him and deceive you, while you have never killed any of my men, have never taken any of my women, and have never harmed me? Particularly you, Colonel Largeau, have treated me well. That is unforgettable. We have never heard from you a word that was false or not serious. God bless you; God bless you. I will not fall so low that I would put you to shame in front of the French.[39]

Bakhit's correspondence with 'Ali Dinar—preserved in particular for the years 1914 and 1915—shows how Bakhit, tactfully but uncompromisingly, continued to deny 'Ali Dinar's claims of suzerainty. It also shows how closely the ruling houses of Dar Sila and Dar Fur were linked; alongside matters of government and kingship, and along with private business arrangements, figure the homesick Fur princesses in Goz Beida and Daju royal wives sending presents (of slaves and livestock) to their beloved daughters in al-Fashir.[40] Relations between the two sultans seem to have returned to what they had been a decade before, in particular when the French, in August 1914, evacuated the garrison of Goz Beida in furthering their war effort against the Germans in Cameroun. The tone of Bakhit's letters to the Fur sultan did not become submissive until 1915, just before the French prepared to reconquer Dar Sila by force of arms. When the French invasion materialized in 1916 and Bakhit fled to Dar Fur, however, 'Ali Dinar was a fugitive himself and could hence not be of help to him. Bakhit returned to the borders of his kingdom, where he was captured.[41] With his exile to Fort Lamy, the precolonial period in Dar Sila inexorably came to an end.

The Initial Impact of Colonial Rule

Until the arrival of the garrison in 1912, Sultan Bakhit was pleased about having had the foresight to contact the French himself and not too worried about the treaty he had signed. It was disconcerting that the new overlords were not Muslims and operated according to a code foreign to him, but, as long as they were distant overlords, these novelties could safely be ignored. With the arrival of the garrison, a more direct confrontation became inevitable. The presence of the foreign soldiers in their newly built fort was a serious blow to Bakhit's prestige and a check upon his actions; on Bakhit's shoulders rested the odious task of conveying French demands to his entourage and subjects, and of showing at least a semblance of enforcing them. Good relations with the French came to depend on whether he obeyed summons to present himself to the commander of the post, ignored the religious indignation of his *faqihs*, acquiesced in losing his popularity with his subjects to his uncompromising son Dhahab, and sacrificed the interests of his relatives and dignitaries to the French. An incident in the marketplace of Goz Beida epitomizes Bakhit's quandary. A French lieutenant who had the arrogance and bad taste to do his marketing on horseback was attacked by a Daju man. The latter failed to put the lieutenant to the knife, but succeeded in indecently exposing him before being caught. Bakhit did not hesitate and had the man, who was the husband of his sister, publicly executed.[42]

Bakhit not only alienated his entourage; he also began to lose control over the nomadic tribes, who tried to play the French against him and besieged the French commander with complaints about his rule. Another group that enjoyed special French protection was the host of foreigners (mostly West Africans) who came to Goz Beida in the wake of the troops in order to cater to French needs.[43] Goz Beida became a "Tower of Babel" (as a French officer expressed it), that is to say, a foreign enclave that was in practice, if not officially, out of Bakhit's control.[44] Finally there were the slaves. The French may not have abolished slavery in this period and may have (reluctantly) condoned the slave trade, but they did establish precedents that made it quite clear to the Daju nobility that disciplining their slaves was becoming more and more difficult. When Hababa Koma, a royal wife, tried to recover slaves who had run away, the French declared them free and refused to let her take action to recover them.[45]

Bakhit's submission to the French not only eroded his authority over his people, but also sapped his material wealth. The largest French demand was the annual tax he had to pay. This tax (al-kharaj) had been fixed at 15,000 francs, but in reality Bakhit had made an oral agreement that he would pay half of his revenue from the animal tax, that is to say, half of (roughly) one-third of the animal wealth of his subjects. In 1912 the French reconsidered their policy, and Bakhit wrote them a letter to complain and explain:

> The reason of this letter is the tax which exists between us and you. In the past [the] Colonel fixed it for us at 5000 *riyal* and we wrote you a letter because *riyal* ar not used by us. Subsequently you fixed our tax at one hundred excellent horses. Know that this is not part of the stipulations agreed upon with Colonels Largeau and Milot.

All the French officials who came here or corresponded with us had only one work (policy), Bakhit continued:

> namely that we take one cow from [every] thirty, one goat from

[every] thirty, and one donkey from [every] thirty; this is the produce of our country. Subsequently we take half for ourselves and send half to the rulers. This is what we agreed upon with them, and they told us: . . . no one will come to you for the sake of that [the tax], but only for the sake of greeting you. All this is known to God. . . . Know that my country is small and that I cannot raise what you have imposed upon me. . . . Why do you impose upon me something that I cannot comply with? Accept from me what we are able to raise: every year one hundred cows will come to you and one thousand goats; that is what we propose, in accordance with the well known stipulation. Let it be known that our country yields to us only cows from nomads, and goats, donkeys and *tukkiyyas* from Daju, nothing more. Taxes can only come from what exists (*al-kharaj ma yakhruj illa min al-mawjud*).[46]

If one realizes that one cow was valued at about 30 or 35 francs, Bakhit's offer might seem to be quite reasonable.

The tax was not Bakhit's only financial obligation to the French. Before and after 1912 he had to provide food, transport, and accommodation to reconnaissance expeditions that toured the country to describe it geographically, and to locate and count its villages. He catered only temporarily for the garrison, which soon grew its own crops, bought grain in the market or requisitioned it from the Daju. But Bakhit did send occasional gifts of honey and butter, as his own Sudanic political code required.[47]

More important than these taxes and services was—from hindsight—the revenue that Bakhit lost, not to the French directly but as a result of their presence. The treaty had stipulated: "the roads will be open for the traders and all the commoners." This was—whether the French realized it or not—a revolutionary demand. It officially put an end to royal control of the long-distance trade, which had until then provided the ruling class with the prestige goods distinguishing it from the commoners. Initially the loss of revenue in taxes, tolls, and greeting gifts traditionally paid by the traders may have been the most obvious result of the French measure. Soon its social impact made itself felt; when imports began to be sold and bought by anyone who had wealth (and particularly cash), the garrison and the new foreign middle class that grew up in its shadow came to possess and even to control the traditional emblems of noble status.

This result of colonial occupation was not unique in Dar Sila. In neighboring Dar Masalit the British occupation created a similar foreign enclave that introduced the beginnings of a cash economy into a country used to barter and to a royally regulated foreign trade.

> The immediate result [of the introduction of coined money] has been a 50 percent depreciation in the cash value of "tokaki" [*tukkiyyas*]. It is now practically true that nothing can be bought here except for cash. The standard of living has completely altered. The households of the well-paid soldiers and police are examples which give rise, in the other inhabitants, to many "wants," formerly unfelt, which the new market, with a score of foreign traders, can supply. Those who formerly wore homespun now call for Manchester goods. Tea, coffee, sugar and other foods are craved for by people who had barely tasted any of them a few years ago.[48]

If this was to some extent true for the commoners, it was even more true for the nobility and the sultan. While Bakhit's income fell in value, he had to keep up with the conspicuous consumption of the "nouveaux riches." The only solution to the sultan's penury, a salary in cash, never seems to have been considered by the French.

Slave-raiding and trading, and cattle-raiding beyond the state's borders were other traditional sources of income that were threatened by the French. However, although the French presence in Goz Beida—where all news and gossip came together—cramped Bakhit's style, the raiding and trading of slaves and cattle continued until after the reconquest of 1916. Bakhit gained an even firmer grip upon the slave trade, which became centered upon his palace, whence the caravans of slave merchants were escorted to the state's borders.[49] However, the new urban middle class that was subservient to the

French had no choice but to demand cash rather than slaves for its goods. The extent to which the nobility could use slaves to buy imports therefore became more limited.

The French did not always recognize the gravity of the impact of their demands. They did not realize that their treatment of Bakhit undermined the only possible alternative to direct military administration. They did not seem (or care) to take into account that the agricultural surplus of Dar Sila was limited and that diverting its flow upset the traditional relations of authority. They were not aware of the revolutionary impact of their demand to "open the roads" and of the emergence of the small foreign merchant class that they brought into being. The lack of Arabic knowledge of most of the commanders in Goz Beida made them even more distrustful of Bakhit than the latter's opportunism and wavering justified. With the exception of the odd commander (such as Capt. Simonet), French policy showed little vision.[50] This lack of insight—so obvious from hindsight—may have partly resulted from the limited vision and training of the French military personnel. Its major cause lay, however, in the prevailing ideology of the colonial age, which presented the conquerors of Africa as the exponents of a great civilizing mission, rather than as the carriers of capitalism.

Epilogue

Throughout the Dar Fur-Wadai region, under different (British and French) political regimes, the economic developments of the first two decades of the twentieth century pointed in the same direction: the introduction of a cash economy and the incorporation of the precolonial states into the world economic system dominated by Europe.[51] In Dar Sila the precolonial (and precapitalist) system was given a reprieve from August 1914 (the evacuation of Goz Beida) to May 1916 (the reconquest). After the reconquest, however, the same process, but now accelerated, was set into motion again.

Although the availability of sugar, tea, cloth, etc. was one factor that drew people into the money economy, the most potent force was—in Dar Sila as elsewhere in the region—the introduction of taxes in cash. As early as 1909

Colonel Millot had insisted that taxes be paid in cash, since this was "the most effective means of determining activity in [commercial] transactions and of stimulating the sluggishness of the taxpayer."[52] However, demanding that people pay in money did not give them money to pay with. In 1917, one year after taxes in cash had been introduced, it was reported that "money is still rare in Sila, for what is spent by the troops is almost entirely siphoned off by the merchants."[53] Whether money was scarce or not, the Daju had to pay. Those who had an agricultural surplus (grain, livestock, cotton cloth) obtained money for taxes by selling this surplus in the market at whatever price the particular circumstances of supply and demand would dictate. Since they usually did not sell until the day to pay taxes had drawn near and the demand for money was great, they usually paid dearly for it.[54]

The new taxation weighed heavily upon the people, partly because the traditional taxes continued to be levied on the side, but mostly because it was rigid and did not have the built-in famine relief of the traditional taxes.[55] This rigidity had grave consequences in times of crisis, such as the natural disasters and crop failures of the 1920s and 1930s, and the economic recession of the early 1930s. The inhabitants of Dar Sila responded in different ways to the new demands for cash. They tried to grow money crops of chillies, onions, or tobacco. They tried to borrow money from the traders, although the latter tended to use their economic leverage over them to increase their political power.[56] They left the country and fled to Dar Fur, where taxes in cash were late in coming and, when introduced, remained lower.[57] They also tried to work for wages and since wage labor was hard to come by in Dar Sila, they migrated east to work on the cotton plantations of the British Nile Valley, went west to work at the French railroads, or enlisted in the French army. [58] Until this day labor migration has continued to be a dominant characteristic of the economy of Dar Sila and its neighbors.

The detailed analysis of the impact of colonial rule in Dar Sila lies beyond the scope of this essay. However, it is evident from the above that from 1916 onwards colonial rule had begun to revolutionize the political and economic order of this distant corner of the French Empire, with grim consequences for rulers and commoners alike.

Notes

1. This is an updated version of the article that appeared in *Cahiers d'Etudes Africaines*, Vol. XXIII (4), No. 92, pp. 447–470. I am grateful to the editors of the journal for permission to reprint it. I gratefully acknowledge financial support from the Netherlands Foundation for the Advancement of Tropical Research (WOTRO). The archival sources on which this article is based are from the Archives nationales, section outre-mer (ANSOM), Aix-en-Provence; the Service historique de l'armée de terre (SHAT), Paris; the Bibliothèque de l'Institut de France (BIF), Paris; and the British colonial archives and archives left by the Mahdist state that are kept in the National Records Office (NRO), Khartoum.

2. Paul Doornbos and M. Lionel Bender, "Languages of Wadai-Darfur," in M. Lionel Bender, ed., *Nilo-Saharan Language Studies*. East Lansing: African Studies Center, Michigan State University, 1983, pp. 43–79. Dar Sila lies between 11° 45' and 12° 15' latitude and 22° 15' and 22° 45' east longitude. In 1961 it had approximately 38,000 inhabitants, of whom 24,000 were Daju, 3,000 Sinyar, and 10,500 Arabic-speaking nomads (SHAT, Tchad, 20/5).

3. For more on Daju traditions of origin, see Henri Berre, *Sultans dadjo du Sila (Tchad)*, Paris: Centre National de la Récherche Scientifique, 1985, pp. 5–18; NRO, Khartoum, Darfur 1/33/17; and SHAT, Tchad, 9: Carnet de Poste Sila, 1912–37 [hereafter: Carnet de Poste Sila].

4. Carnet de Poste Sila; H.A. MacMichael, *A History of the Arabs in the Sudan*. Cambridge: Cambridge University Press, 1922, Vol. 1, p. 74; NRO Khartoum, Mahdiyya 2/37, doc. 35.

5. Berre, *Sultans dadjo*, pp. 49–57; SHAT, Tchad, 3/2; and SHAT, Tchad, 4: Colonne du Sila, 21 May 1916 [hereafter: Colonne du Sila]. Compare Lidwien Kapteijns, *Mahdist Faith and Sudanic Tradition: The History of the Masalit Sultanate, 1870–1930*. London: Routledge and Kegan Paul, 1985, pp. 33, 48–61.

6. SHAT, Tchad, 3/2.

7. *Ibid.* Il n'existe comme organisation politique que le bon plaisir du sultan entouré de ses frères, de ses fils et de nombreux fonctionnaires.

8. Berre, *Sultans dadjo*, pp. 41–46; BIF, Manuscript: Capt. Simonet, "Rapport de Reconnaissance sur les Confins du Sila (Goz Beida, 28 Juillet 1914)" [hereafter:

Simonet, "Rapport"]; and compare Kapteijns, *Mahdist Faith*, pp. 137–144, 166–167.

9. Berre, *Sultans dadjo*, pp. 33–40; Colonne du Sila; and compare Kapteijns, *Mahdist Faith*, pp. 147–152.

10. *Ibid.*

11. Berre. *Sultans dadjo*, pp. 33–40; Colonne du Sila; and compare Kapteijns, *Mahdist Faith*, pp. 144–152.

12. Berre, *Sultans dadjo*, pp. 33–40, 49–57; and SHAT, Tchad, 3/3. In 1916 some of the slave villages on the Bahr Azum, a very fertile area, had been 500 and 700 huts, while most villages had between 100 and 200 huts. The villages belonged to either the sultan or other dignitaries of state. When the French conquered Dar Sila in 1916, many of these slaves fled back to their home countries to the south and west of Dar Sila (Colonne du Sila).

13. Berre, *Sultans dadjo*, pp. 41–46; Colonne du Sila; and compare Kapteijns, *Mahdist Faith*, pp. 147–148, 158–159.

14. Compare Lidwien Kapteijns and Jay Spaulding, "Precolonial Trade between States in the Eastern Sudan, c.1700–c.1900," in *African Economic History*, No. 11 (1982), pp. 29–62.

15. For the hunting parties, see SHAT, Tchad, 3/2 (25 October 1913); and Lidwien Kapteijns and Jay Spaulding, *After the Millennium: Diplomatic Correspondence from Wadai and Dar Fur on the Eve of Colonial Conquest, 1885–1916.* East Lansing: African Studies Center, Michigan State University, 1988, pp. 350–355, 438–442, 502–504, 534–539. For slave raiding, see Berre, *Sultans dadjo*, pp. 15–18; SHAT, Tchad, 3/2 (11 July 1911); and interviews with descendants of the Sinyar ruling family, Dar Sinyar, 7 May 1979.

16. Lidwien Kapteijns and al-Hadi Ahmad, "The Chado-Sudanese Frontier on the Eve of Colonial Conquest," in *Sudan Texts Bulletin*, 3 (1982), pp. 59–61, 68–69.

17. Kapteijns and Spaulding, *After the Millennium*, pp. 438–442.

18. Kapteijns and Spaulding, *After the Millennium*, pp. 456–459, 485–491.

19. G. Nachtigal, *Sahara and Sudan*, Vol. IV: Wadai and Darfur, translated by A.G.B. and H.J. Fisher, Berkeley: University of California Press, 1971, pp. 75, 81, 346–347, 359; Le Cheikh Mohammed Ebn-Omar El-Tounsy, *Voyage au Ouadây*, translated by N. Perron, Paris: Benjamin Duprat, 1851, map; and idem, *Voyage*

au Darfour, translated by N. Perron, Paris; Benjamin Duprat, 1845, map.

20. Kapteijns, *Mahdist Faith*, pp. 65.

21. Kapteijns, *Mahdist Faith*, pp. 83–94.

22. NRO, Mahdiyya, 1/13 III, doc. 275 (8 Ramadan 1309/6 April 1890).

23. Berre, *Sultans dadjo*, p. 19–30; Simonet, "Rapport"; Carnet de Poste Sila; and compare Kapteijns, *Mahdist Faith*, p. 17.

24. Kapteijns and Spaulding, *After the Millennium*, pp. 406–415.

25. For the slaves, see Berre, *Sultans dadjo*, pp. 33–40; Carnet de Poste Sila; and Colonne du Sila. For the refugees, see SHAT, Tchad, 3/2 (7 march 1917). For the pilgrims, see J.S. Birks, *Across the Savannas to Mecca: The Overland Pilgrimage Route from West Africa*. Totowa, NJ: Frank Cass, 1978, pp. 103–104; and NRO Khartoum, Darfur 1/33/169 (July 1911). For pilgrims and traders, see Simonet, "Rapport"; ANSOM, Tchad, I, 7 (January 1912).

26. Kapteijns, *Mahdist Faith*, pp. 112–113, 121.

27. Kapteijns, *Mahdist Faith*, p. 63; and Simonet, "Rapport."

28. Kapteijns and Spaulding, *After the Millennium*, pp. 485–491. For Abu'l-Khayrat, see Kapteijns, *Mahdist Faith*, pp. 96–97; and Musa al-Mubarak al-Hasan, *Tarikh Dar Fur al-Siyasi*, Khartoum: Khartoum University Press, n.d. [1970], pp. 164, 171–172.

29. Kapteijns and Spaulding, *After the Millennium*, pp. 485–491. See also Musa al-Mubarak, *Tarikh*, pp. 183–185; and Kapteijns, *Mahdist Faith*, p. 101.

30. Simonet, "Rapport."

31. Interview with the wife of Amir Bahr al-Din 'Ali Dinar, al-Fashir, June 1979.

32. Kapteijns and Spaulding, *After the Millennium*, pp. 438–465, 476–479.

33. Kapteijns and Spaulding, *After the Millennium*, pp. 485–491.

34. Kapteijns and Spaulding, *After the Millennium*, pp. 453–455; and Kapteijns, *Mahdist Faith*, p. 182.

35. Kapteijns, *Mahdist Faith*, p. 184.

36. Berre, *Sultans Dadjo*, p. 40.

37. Kapteijns and Spaulding, *After the Millennium*, pp. 502 ff.

38. Kapteijns and Spaulding, *After the Millennium*, pp. 372–376; and Berre, *Sultans dadjo*, p. 42.

39. Kapteijns and Spaulding, *After the Millennium*, pp. 485–491, 480–484.

40. Kapteijns and Spaulding, *After the Millennium*, pp. 510–512, 516–518, 522–524.

41. For a detailed account of the conquest, see Colonne du Sila and Col. Hilaire, "L'Occupation du Dar Sila: Rapport du Colonel Hilaire sur les operations du 13 au 17 mai 1916 et la réoccupation de Goz Beida," in *Afrique française. Renseignements coloniaux*, XXVII, 5–6, 1917, pp. 105–118.

42. Carnet de Poste Sila.

43. SHAT, Tchad, 3/2 (11 July 1911). Bakhit forbade the Arab tribes to participate in slave-raiding or slave-trading in Dar Kuti and Dar Runga, which were his monopoly. A report in ANSOM, Tchad I, 7 (June 1912) noted that the Fezzan, *jallaba*, and Peul were happy to see the French garrison arrive. That the French favored the merchants is also evident from the fact that they appointed a board of four foreign traders and three foreign holy men to succeed the puppet king of Wadai, who was deposed in 1912 (SHAT, Tchad, 11/3).

44. Simonet, "Rapport"; and SHAT, Tchad, 3/2 (10 September 1916).

45. SHAT, Tchad, 3/2 (2 December 1912).

46. Kapteijns and Spaulding, *After the Millennium*, pp. 469–473.

47. SHAT, Tchad, 3/2. Bakhit was also obliged to collect firearms from his people and hand them over to the French commander.

48. Kapteijns, *Mahdist Faith*, p. 223, quoting the words of R. Davies, Resident of Dar Masalit, in 1924. *Tukkiyyas* are lengths of homespun cotton.

49. SHAT, Tchad, 3/2 (11 July 1911).

50. For the lack of Arabic knowledge, see SHAT, Tchad, 3/2 (Mongelous, 19 August 1912 and 8 July 1913). For Capt. Simonet's insight, see SHAT, Tchad, 3/2 (19 July 1914). As for slavery, the French acted slowly and cautiously once they recognized the significance of their reforms. They freed individual slaves who ran away from their masters. They freed the seventy-five slaves of the Bani Halba who had stayed behind when their masters had fled to Dar Fur (SHAT, Tchad, 3/2 23 February 1917). However, even after the reconquest, the governor of Goz Beida rejected requests for freedom by the slaves of the nobility. He advised them "to continue to work for their masters as in the past, on the condition of the following guarantees: the prohibition against being sold, the prohibition against separating families and taking away children, and the suppression of ill-treatment." He added, "What more could they want for the time being, since most of

the fruits of their labor belong to them? Many are the owners of cattle and donkeys." (Berre, *Sultans dadjo*, p. 53).

51. Compare Kapteijns, *Mahdist Faith*, pp. 208–243.

52. SHAT, Tchad, 8/2 (Millot, 1909): ". . . le moyen le plus efficace pour déterminer l'activité des transactions et stimuler la torpeur du contribuable." Taxation in cash was introduced in Wadai as early as 1911; it was listed as one of the causes of the Kodoi rebellion of June—August 1911 (ANSOM, Tchad I, 7).

53. SHAT, Tchad, 3/2 (25 February 1917): ". . . l'argent est encore rare dans le Sila, celui dépensé par les troupes étant presque entièrement drainé par les commerçants."

54. Carnet de Poste Sila: "Only at the time of taxation does one see sums of money circulate in the market." For details on the taxes levied in 1916–17, see SHAT, Tchad, 3/2 (10 September 1916 and 23 February 1917).

55. Kapteijns, *Mahdist Faith*, pp. 230–231. The most important features of the old system were the following: (i) Below a certain minimum crops were tax-exempt. (ii) Taxes were levied from the harvested crop, so that taxes were automatically reduced or remitted when the crops failed. Bakhit's statement that "taxes can only come from what exists" (see note 46) must be seen in this light. (iii) In case of drought or famine, the government opened its reserves of tax grain to the people. In contrast, the French raised taxes throughout the period (1917–1931) irrespective of the droughts and epidemics that occurred. Only in 1932, the third year of continuous crop failures and a year in which the world recession had made money dear, did they distribute food and sowing grain (Carnet de Poste Sila).

56. Berre, *Sultans dadjo*, pp. 62–70.

57. NRO, Khartoum, Darfur 3/1/5.

58. Berre, *Sultans dadjo*, pp. 84–85; and NRO, Khartoum, Darfur 3/1/5 (7 August 1936).

CHAPTER SEVEN

Two Muslims on the Eve of British Colonialism in the Sudan, 1908

JAY SPAULDING

"THE WORST OF HOLY MEN," said a time-tested Sufi maxim, "is the one who visits princes." This thought may well have passed through the minds of many Sudanese religious leaders in the months that followed the spectacular bloodletting of the British reconquest—months that soon lengthened into the first decade of what Christians called the twentieth century. "It is very important that the Government should do nothing which could be interpreted as a sign of weakness," the alien conqueror warned his followers as revolts flared up in diverse quarters, "and all insubordination must be promptly and severely suppressed."[1]

It was. Yet the new regime, aside from its ability to kill large numbers of people expeditiously, was in most other respects very weak, and it lost little time in searching out potential supporters and assistants from among the Sudanese populace. "One of our first tasks," wrote a junior official, "was to compile a register of people who 'mattered' and to whom responsibility could be entrusted."[2]

The pursuit of threats to public order and the search for useful collaborators often led to the same doorstep—that of the village holy man. Would this local dignitary elect to become a dutiful tax-assessor and informer, to be rewarded, perhaps, in due course, with a Robe of Honour/Religious/Third Class? Or would he choose to become one of the leaders of popular resistance, to be crushed "almost mercilessly,"[3] as was the Halawi leader 'Abd al-Qadir in April 1908? The answer usually lay in the specific history of each local community and the internal politics of its religious leadership. Conspicuously, it could be anticipated that those communities whose leaders had affiliated themselves with the Khatmiya Brotherhood as local *khalifas* during the Turkish period would be more sympathetic to the new government than those whose leaders had supported the Mahdi. The practical application of this principle, however, was complicated by the fact that many families of local religious prominence had themselves been divided or equivocal in regard to their political loyalties.

In short, the political orientation of each leader had to be ascertained individually: "Direct personal contact between the governing classes and the governed is the easiest way," advised a government circular of 1905.[4] Thus, as the British rulers gradually consolidated their authority, they demanded that each local religious dignitary make himself visible to the government to be inspected, and then rewarded or disciplined. Few Sudanese religious leaders could evade the necessity, however distasteful, of "visiting the princes" of their day.

Any authoritarian regime profits from the existence of a statute that many or most subjects systematically violate; since all are guilty, anyone may be singled out for punishment at the ruler's discretion. In the early twentieth-century Sudan, perhaps "the most notable instance" of "law out of harmony with native ideas" was the set of regulations introduced to halt the slave trade and ultimately, to end the institution of slavery itself.[5] The question as to who, if anyone, should be singled out for investigation and punishment at any given moment was a particularly sensitive one. "As a young Inspector," wrote one official regarding incidents that began in 1909, "I often found the application of official [slavery] policy to individual cases harrowing and distasteful."[6] Once this administrative decision was made, however, the actual enforcement of regulations could be entrusted to the police; these officers—usually themselves recently liberated ex-slaves—could be relied upon to carry out their assigned duties with wholehearted enthusiasm spiced with revenge. For example, one could send them to summon a reluctant holy man who had failed to present himself before the new government. . . .

Among the many locally prominent religious dignitaries were the 'Ababsa, a family of the Rubatab country that lay along the Nile between the towns of Berber and Abu Hammad. During bygone days of the kingdom of Sinnar, the legendary mid-eighteenth century 'Abbasi leader al-hajj Sa'd[7] had been singled out for special gifts of honor by the Funj Sultan Badi IV.[8] Thereafter, however, the fortunes of the 'Ababsa family had been increasingly overshadowed by local rivals. Conspicuous among these latter was the clan of the last Funj district ruler, the *makk* Abu Hijl; his descendants not only enriched themselves as businessmen and administrators under the Turks, but so skillfully finessed a timely shift in their political allegiance to the cause of the Mahdi that they not only retained their personal fortunes, but placed their incumbent leader Daqrashawi on the seat of power over all the Rubatab country.[9] The 'Ababsa persevered, however, and their finest hour soon followed. By the close of 1885 they had seen Daqrashawi discredited in the eyes of the Khalifa 'Abdallahi, and while Dagrashawi Abu Hijl languished in confinement in Omdurman, the 'Abbasi leader al-Hasan al-hajj Sa'd was appointed in his place as *'amil 'umum* (supreme administrator) over the Rubatab.[10] So it was that the 'Ababsa bore the honor the honor or onus of high responsibility in the Mahdist government at the moment of the British reconquest.

The document translated below is a letter, dated 23 Safar 1326/27 March 1908, addressed to a Sheikh Muhammad al-hajj Sa'd, possibly a brother of the recent Mahdist *'amil 'umum* and perhaps himself the erstwhile subordinate administrator of the Rubatab subdistrict that included the mother *khalwa* of the 'Ababsa at Nadi.[11] The author of the letter does not identify himself; he addresses Sheikh Muhammad *de haut en bas* as "our son," and seems to be rather intimately acquainted with his affairs. The letter begins with the distinctive formulae employed by members of the Khatimya Brotherhood, and Sheikh Muhammad is addressed as a *khalifa*—in this context, a term meaning a local Khatmiya leader. It would follow that either the anonymous writer or Sheikh Muhammad himself were Khatmiya partisans, or that for political reasons they wished to be identified as such should the letter fall into unfriendly hands. The issue at stake in the letter is the apparently inevitable necessity for both men to present themselves before the British authorities, who have been exerting pressure upon them to do so by sending around policemen—ostensibly to ask questions about slaves. The writer explains that he will follow the example of "Our Lord 'Abd al-Rahman," the son of the Mahdi, and surrender. He concludes with the advice that if the British should really turn out to be concerned about slaves, the correct way to deal with the question is to say that the slaves are indebted to their master's establishment for a certain quantity of food. The new rulers of the Sudan, he had learned, might well be eager to liberate slaves, but they could be counted upon never to forgive a debtor.

Translation of the Letter

In the name of God, the Merciful, the Compassionate.
With Him is help at inception and consummation.
The prayers of God be upon our master Muhammad, in essence, attribute
    and name,
[The one] esteemed and revered with every honor.
To the presence of the one we love and accept,
Whom we remember always and do not forget,
For the sight of whom our heart yearns,
Our son the *khalifa*, Sheikh Muhammad al-hajj Sa'd.
May God preserve him.
Amen; then, amen.
We inform Your Presence in regard to the slaves.

The police of al-'Abidiya[12] came to me from the Government and said:

"Come present yourself to the Government because of the slaves."

They say that Our Son should turn himself in, and likewise, that Bint Wad Habud should present herself and surrender.

We will follow Sayyidna 'Abd al-Rahman [al-Mahdi], for how could I refuse to present myself because of my status, and because it is your presence and the sight of you that are expected (for the matter is entrusted to you), when the slaves desire [even] his presence?

The police said to me:

"If you remain, and do not come present yourself, I will blot out his face!"

I will say to the Government:

"I have made the journey to her [the Government's] people, and am now present with the Son of the Sheikh ['Abd al-Rahman, the son of the Mahdi].

If you asks about the slaves, they are carrying from his compound [owe him] 200 *qilada* of dates, an *ardab* of wheat, and a half-*ardab* of *dhurra*."

Peace
23 Safar 1326
[27 March 1908]

Notes

1. Lord Kitchener's "Memorandum to Mudirs" of 1899. See John Obert Voll, "A History of the Khatmiyyah Tariqah in the Sudan," Ph.D. dissertation, Department of History, Harvard University (1969), II, 344.

2. H.C. Jackson, *Sudan Days and Ways*. London: St. Martin's Press, 1954, p. 44.

3. Governor-General Wingate, 1908. See Muddathir 'Abd al-Rahim, *Imperialism and nationalism in the Sudan*. Oxford: Clarendon Press, 1969, p. 90.

4. E. Bonham-Carter, in the Annual Report of 1905. See Voll, "History," II, 339.

5. Lord Cromer, in the Annual Report of 1902. See Voll, "History," II, 339, note 40.

6. Jackson, *Days and Ways*, p. 43.

7. For the mighty deeds of al-hajj Sa'd, see 'Abdallahi 'Ali Ibrahim and Ahmad 'Abd al-Rahim Nasr, *Min Adab al-Rubatab al-Sha'bi* (Khartoum, 1968), pp. 28–30.

8. Ahmad al-Mu'tasim al-'Abbas, 'Ali 'Osman Muhammad Salih and Jay Spaulding, "A Colophon from Eighteenth-Century Sinnar," *Fontes Historiae Africanae: Bulletin d'Information*, VI (1981), 13–18.

9. Jay Spaulding, "The Life and Times of al-Rabb Jad, a Nineteenth-Century Sudanese Freedman," in *Sudan Texts Bulletin*, VI (1984), 44–50.

10. The Khalifa 'Abdallahi wrote a lengthy but undated letter to al-Hasan Sa'd in his capacity as leader of the Rubatab: See Sudan Archive, Universitetet i Bergen, NI 125.11/27. A letter of 19 Rabi'I 1303/26 December 1885 (from the private collection of Mr. Jon Graves) reveals al-Hasan al-hajj Sa'd in his capacity as *'amil umum*, appointing a subordinate "Sheikh Muhammad" (possible the recipient of the present letter) and enjoining the prompt collection of taxes. A copy of both of these documents has been deposited with the National Records Office in Khartoum.

11. Sudan Archive, Universitetet i Bergen, NI 118.11/20.

12. A small town at the southern border of the Rubatab country, between Berber and the probable residence of Sheikh Muhammad at Nadi.

Index

Amharic, Oromo and Somali names are indexed by first name, i.e. Muhammad Ali appears under M, Godana Babbo under G, and Takla Giyorgis appears under T. When a name is commonly preceded by an honorific, it is indexed accordingly, i.e. Sayyid Muhammad Abdille Hasan appears under S, Sheikh Uways under S, and Abba Jifar under A. All other names are indexed by surname.

Turkiyya, period of Turkish rule in
the Sudan, 1820–1883 125, 126

'Ulama, men of learning 41, 45
Ulama 107, 108
Ulama 94–95
'Ulla, son of sultan Ishaq Abu Risha of
Dar Sila 128
Ullendorff 103, 104
Ummah, Arabic for Muslim communi-
ty 4–5
'Uthman Digna 35
Uways al–Barawi, Shaykh 12, 25
Uways Muhammad, see Sheikh Uways
Uways, see Sheikh Uways
Uwaysiya, muslim brotherhood 6, 36,
48–54

Wadaad 11, 12
Wadaad kitaab Gaab 53, 66
Wadaad(s), Somali Muslim religious
man 36–37, 38
Wadai, large sultanate in eastern Chad
117, 118, 119, 121, 124, 125,
126, 127, 129, 130, 131, 132,
133, 134
Wadi al-Masha'ikh 27
Wage labor appears in Dar Sila 141
Wahhab(i) 54
Wahhabi(s), Muslim doctrine 36, 42,
44
Wahhabiya 55
Waj 78
Waliya Allah 70
Wallo 106, 108
Wallo Muslims 8
Walqayit 109
Warra Himano 85–86, 91–93

Warrenleh, spearbearer 37
Warsangali 59
Al-Warsangali, Muhammad B. Yusuf
44
Webi Shebelle 25
West Africans in Dar Sila 123, 137
Wilaya 26

Yajju 83, 94
Yaman 12, 14
Yemen 104
Yifaq 109
Yohannis I (Emperor) 105
Yohannes IV (Emperor), see also Yo-
hannis 8
Yusuf, sultan of Wadai (1874–1898)
131
Yussuf Ahmad Tayimu 113, 114, 115

Zaghawa, ethnic group of eastern
Chad and western Sudan 125
Zakah tax on grain and livestock in
Dar Sila 122
Zamzam, Well of 21
Zanzibar 37, 49
Zawiya, see Juma'a
Zaydis 12
Zayla' 12, 16, 25, 49
Zayla'iya Brotherhood 17, 18
Zayli'i also Zeyli'i 36, 38
Zayli'i, see Sheikh 'Abdirahman al-
Zayli'i 8
Zayli'i, Abdul-Rahman 50–53
Zewde Gabre-Sellassie 106
Zizyphus Spina 19
Al-Zugbar Rahma, Sudanese slaver
and warlord 125